C

R.F. Langley was born i̲ educated at Jesus College, Cambridge, and taught English and Art History at secondary schools in the Midlands. He lived in Staffordshire for most of his life, but in 1999 retired to Suffolk, a county that inspired much of his work. His *Collected Poems* (2000) was shortlisted for the Whitbread Prize for Poetry and 'To a Nightingale' (2010), his last published poem, won the Forward Prize for Best Single Poem. He died in 2011.

Jeremy Noel-Tod lives in Norfolk and teaches Literature and Creative Writing at the University of East Anglia. His poetry criticism has been widely published, and he was the revising editor of the *Oxford Companion to Modern Poetry* (2013).

Also by R.F. Langley from Carcanet Press

The Face of It (2007)
Collected Poems (2000)

R.F. LANGLEY

Complete Poems

edited by
Jeremy Noel-Tod

CARCANET

First published in Great Britain in 2015 by

Carcanet Press Limited
Alliance House
Cross Street
Manchester
M2 7AQ

www.carcanet.co.uk

We welcome your comments on our publications
Write to us at info@carcanet.co.uk

A CIP catalogue record for this book is available from the British Library

ISBN 978 1 784100 64 3

The publisher acknowledges financial assistance from Arts Council England

Typeset by XL Publishing Services, Exmouth
Printed and bound in England by SRP Ltd, Exeter

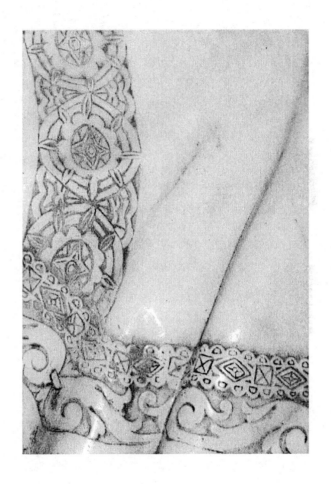

Detail from Nicholas Stone's memorial monument
to Arthur and Elizabeth Coke, St Andrew's church,
Bramfield, Suffolk (1634).

Contents

Introduction

The poetry of R.F. Langley is a distinctively English flowering of the modernist tradition in verse – a tradition, it seems to propose, that runs from Shakespeare to J.H. Prynne via Samuel Taylor Coleridge and Gerard Manley Hopkins. Accurate in everything, including etymology (Latin: *accurare*, from *cura*, care), Langley's writing honours its own motto that 'nothing is less than / particular'. Never written in haste or to order, it readily won the admiration of other poets, and, over three decades, a wider readership. This book contains all the poems that Langley intended for publication, along with his bibliographic notes on their sources. Set beside the more prolific writings of his peers, it is not an extensive body of work. But there are few oeuvres published this century that can rival it for intensity of perception or perfection of finish.

Roger Francis Langley was born in Rugby, Warwickshire, on 23 October 1938. He was the eldest son of Frederick ('Lofty') Langley, a school teacher, and his wife, Agnes ('Sis'), who fostered in all their children an enthusiasm for natural history and hands-on hobbies. Describing with relish an acorn picked up on a country walk, Langley remembered how 'my mother used to give me them when she pushed me down the lane in my pram'.[1] During the war, his father served as an airframe mechanic in Kenya, sending home illustrated letters that left a lasting impression. A lifelong cherisher of pocketable treasures, Langley preserved into adulthood his collections of cigarette cards, animal figurines, and Dinky wartime vehicles.

The family lived in Aldridge, Staffordshire, near the town of Walsall, where Langley and his brothers, Peter and Timothy, attended Queen Mary's Grammar School. In 1957, he went to Jesus College, Cambridge, on an open scholarship to study for the English Tripos. At Jesus he met Jeremy (J.H.) Prynne, with whom he formed a close friendship. In their final year, Langley and Prynne were supervised by the poet and critic Donald Davie. On graduation, inspired by the poetry of Ezra Pound and the art writing of Adrian Stokes (to which Davie had introduced them), they bought an old greengrocer's delivery van and undertook a tour of Southern France and Northern Italy to study Renaissance art and architecture.

Langley had been encouraged by the literary critic Frank

Kermode, then at the University of Manchester, to go on to postgraduate study of Shakespeare. Instead, he took a pragmatic decision to train as a secondary school teacher. Returning to the West Midlands he began work at Shire Oak Grammar, Brownhills, Walsall in 1961, moving to Wolverhampton Grammar in 1965, and then Bishop Vesey's Grammar, Sutton Coldfield, in 1980, where he became Head of English. An inspirational teacher, Langley is remembered fondly by former students, who were impressed by his diversely avant-garde curriculum – Ezra Pound, Samuel Beckett, William Carlos Williams, Jean-Paul Sartre, Melanie Klein – and his exacting but encouraging manner. A week's lessons might be given over to examining the implications of the opening line of a Shakespeare play, or a writing exercise might be set on whatever was in your pockets. He especially enjoyed devising creative lessons for the younger classes as well as preparing sixth-formers for university-level study. A profound believer in the patient appreciation of artistic technique, he also gave extra-curricular Art History evening classes at home to pupils and local people.

After a brief first marriage, in 1972 he married Barbara, who also taught at Wolverhampton Grammar. The couple settled in the Staffordshire village of Shenstone, near Lichfield, and had two children, Ruth (b. 1974) and Eric (b. 1977). The family often went on holiday to Suffolk, where Langley took pleasure in visiting the county's medieval churches – in particular Holy Trinity, Blythburgh and St Andrew's, Westhall. These buildings became important locations for the reflective prose of his journals, which he began in 1969. As his poetry came to be better known, a selection of journal entries was published in the poetry magazine *PN Review* and then as a volume with Shearsman Books in 2006. Reviewers compared Langley's prose to that of the greatest English nature writers: Dorothy Wordsworth, Gerard Manley Hopkins, Richard Jefferies, and J.A. Baker. Hopkins had been his favourite poet at school and Nigel Wheale, a pupil who became a lifelong friend, remembers that the example of the Victorian poet's journals was 'absolutely central' to Langley's teaching and thinking in the early 1960s. At that time, Langley was also an active draughtsman and painter, who made painstaking studies of the natural world inspired by the Pre-Raphaelite painters, as well as Vorticist-style portraits.

Pound was at this point, he said, 'the centre of my universe'.[2]

But he only began to write verse in earnest when he 'found out about [contemporary] American poetry'. Picking up Donald Allen's anthology *New American Poetry* (1960), he responded to a new model of the intensity and energy that poetic writing might achieve.[3] The meditative concentration and precise *mise en page* of the first poem he preserved, 'Matthew Glover', evinces the influence of Charles Olson, whose poem 'The Kingfishers' Langley taught to his sixth-form pupils. Olson and other post-Poundian poets in the anthology, such as Ed Dorn and Robert Creeley, were important points of orientation for the Cambridge-based 'worksheet' *The English Intelligencer* (1966–68). This mimeographed magazine, edited by the poets Andrew Crozier and Peter Riley, was circulated by request to interested readers, including Langley. He also remained in correspondence with Prynne, who had befriended Dorn and Olson while studying in the States.

Langley began publishing poetry in 1978 with a pamphlet, *Hem*, from *infernal methods*, a small press run by Nigel Wheale. In 1994, he collected all his verse to date in another *infernal methods* book, *Twelve Poems*. His sixtieth birthday was marked by a festschrift of poems, *Sneak's Noise* (1998) – the allusion is to *Henry IV, Part 2*, 2.4 – which contained contributions from friends and fellow poets, including Thomas A. Clark, Roy Fisher, Helen Macdonald, Douglas Oliver, and Peter Riley. The following year saw the appearance of *Collected Poems*, which was published by Carcanet and shortlisted for the Whitbread (now the Costa) Prize for Poetry.

In 1999, Langley retired from teaching and moved with Barbara to Bramfield, a small village near the town of Halesworth in Suffolk. He had first gone here with Jeremy Prynne to admire Nicholas Stone's memorial sculpture of Elizabeth Coke (d. 1627), who became the subject of one of his earliest poems, 'The Ecstasy Inventories'. In the lanes and nature reserves of Suffolk he pursued his interests in entomology and ornithology. Holidays to Italy, meanwhile, allowed him to renew first-hand his knowledge of Renaissance art, and to examine buildings, sculptures, and paintings that for years he had known only as photographic plates and slides. He also spent time studying the nearby art collections at the Sainsbury Centre for Visual Arts and the Norwich Castle Museum. Writing verse more regularly than ever before, he published new poems in *PN Review* and the *London Review of Books*, and travelled to give readings.

In 2010 Langley was diagnosed with prostate cancer and underwent radiotherapy treatment at the Norfolk and Norwich University Hospital. He died suddenly of heart failure at home in Bramfield on 25 January 2011. Later that year he was posthumously awarded the Forward Prize for Best Single Poem, 'To a Nightingale'. The title of the poem indicates Langley's affinities with the English Romantic poets, and in particular Wordsworth and Coleridge (who composed a 'conversation' poem on 'The Nightingale'). Writing to the critic Ian Brinton in October 2010, he commented: 'I would guess my deepest feelings have always been for Coleridge's Conversation Poems, the Lime Tree Bower, the shock which begins where the particular strikes, beyond any general concepts, geographical, historical or whatever.'[4] Discussing his work shortly before he died, he said he thought of his own poems as 'odes' in this tradition.

At the back of the first of three notebooks in which Langley recorded the diverse sources of his verse is a quotation from the philosopher Thomas Nagel, which catches the philosophical puzzle that runs through all his writing:

[The] incredulity that one should be anyone in particular, a specific individual of a particular species existing at a particular time and place in the universe.[5]

Wordsworthian joy or wonder at the world was, he said in interview, 'the chief thing [...] the thing I value'.[6] In a letter to another former pupil and friend, Andrew Brewerton, Langley remarked with dry humour on the outline of his career when presented in the form of a brief, factual biography:

The curriculum vitae looks more like a curriculum mortis to me! Maybe I ought to include peripheral study of spiders and Nicholas Stone, hours spent in hides on Blyth Estuary, standing in the south nave aisle in St Philibert, Tournus, crashed out in the square at Dragoman eating spaghetti and raspberry jam, listening to Donald Davie, listening to JHP, staggering round Urbino, having a sore throat in front of the Rubens in Munich, watching the Perseids from Dunwich beach etc.

Standing still and attending to a landscape, a creature, an artwork was Langley's way of getting through, as he said, 'to what was really there'.[7] Jeremy Prynne, his companion on many walks, recalls it as 'a kind of mental and indeed moral photography':

> His alertness to perception was enhanced by a studied practice of taking up an immobile, silent stance, either inside a building or upon some grassy bank outside, to open his gaze and thoughts over an extended period, mind busy with interior responses or purposefully blank, to tune in to his surroundings.

In all his looking – the spectacles he wore for myopia taken off, in a characteristic gesture, to allow for close, unimpeded focusing – it might be said that Langley sought the truth of John Ruskin's remark that

> The greatest thing a human soul ever does in this world is to *see* something, and tell what it *saw* in a plain way. Hundreds of people can talk for one who can think, but thousands can think for one who can see. To see clearly is poetry, prophecy, and religion – all in one.[8]

As Prynne put it during the memorial service held at St Andrew's church, Bramfield, on 12 February 2011:

> [For Roger,] the smallest things were absolutely everything – if you knew the difference between a martin and a swift you knew everything – not just something – you knew the whole universal truth of things if you knew one thing deeply and exactly and carefully.[9]

When Langley's death was announced in a brief note by Peter Riley to the UKPoetry email list, it drew a number of tributes. Among them was the following poem by Michael Haslam, which casts Langley as Hodge, the labouring Everyman of the English countryside, and a diminutive form of 'Roger'. Haslam imagines the 'Master' poet mourned by his own invented sprite, Jack:

> What's that I read? Is Hodge
> The Master dead? I thought I heard
> what Peter Riley said rise from a simper
> to a wail, and thought I saw the bird-like
> spirit-imp of mischief, Man Jack ipse, sat
> upon a doorstep with a spotted handkerchief
> before his face, and a discarded hat.

How could a heart like Roger's fail
with such a knave as Jack to set the pace?
The case is grave, and yet it's not too glib to state
that through observant wit, throughout the poetry
of R.F. Langley, the spirit lives.

The liberating discovery of 'Man Jack' as an imaginative surrogate
in the early nineties, and the poems that followed – after almost
a decade's silence – clearly mark the start of the second and more
prolific half of Langley's career, in which he composed with greater
fluency and an increasingly direct use of the first-person voice.
There is no need, however, to propose narratives of development
or progression. From first to last, R.F. Langley wrote finely
concentrated, magically animated poems on the profound mysteries
of perception, contemplation, memory, and the person, that will
endure as long as the language they so lovingly employ.

Jeremy Noel-Tod

Notes

1 'From a Journal' [14 October 2007], *PN Review*, 181 (May–June 2008), p. 12.
2 Quoted in Charles Mundye, 'Roger Langley – An Appreciation', *PN Review*, 199 (May–June 2011), p. 17.
3 'R.F. Langley Interviewed by R.F. Walker', in *Don't Start Me Talking* (Cambridge: Salt, 2006), ed. Tim Allen and Andrew Duncan, pp. 237–57 (p. 239).
4 Ian Brinton, 'Charles Olson and Poetry in England', *Tears in the Fence*, 53 (2011), pp. 108–117 (p. 108).
5 Thomas Nagel, 'Subjective and Objective', in *Mortal Questions* (Cambridge: Cambridge University Press, 1979), pp. 196–213 (p. 206).
6 'R.F. Langley Interviewed', p. 246.
7 'R.F. Langley Interviewed', p. 254.
8 *Modern Painters* (1856), ed. David Barrie (London: André Deutsch, 1987), p. 404.
9 Quoted in Tom Lowenstein, 'Roger Langley 23 October 1938–25 January 2011', *PN Review*, 200, June–July 2011, pp. 12–13.

Acknowledgements

The introduction to this volume could not have been written without material kindly provided by three people who knew Roger Langley well over many years: Andrew Brewerton, Jeremy Prynne, and Nigel Wheale. I would like to thank them all, along with David Mills, who read and commented on my prefatory essay to the notes. Anyone researching R.F. Langley's life and work begins with the interview conducted by Bob (R.H.) Walker, first published in 1996 by Andrew Duncan in *Angel Exhaust* magazine. I am grateful to Michael Haslam for permission to print his memorial verses, as posted on 11 January 2011 to the UKPoetry listserv maintained by Keith Tuma (ukpoetry@listserv.miamioh.edu).

I have benefited from conversations about Langley's writing with Stephen Benson, Peter Gizzi, Leo Mellor, Jack Palmer, Fern Richards, and Michael Schmidt. My late father, Alex Noel-Tod, left some bibliographic notes that I was glad to have. To my wife, Beccy, I am indebted as always for wise advice, encouragement, and more. Eric and Ruth Langley have been ready, helpful, and reassuring advisers throughout the editorial process. My greatest debt is to Barbara Langley, who generously provided all the unpublished material in this volume, and who in its conception and arrangement was co-editor. I would like to repeat, with Roger, the dedication of his *Collected Poems* here: 'For Barbara'. All errors, of course, are mine alone.

Note on the Text

This volume contains all the poems that R.F. Langley published, in the final version that appeared. It also includes one poem that he intended for publication. The order of the book follows the contents list of the folder in which he kept typescript copies of his finished poems (the first two uncollected poems were not included in this folder, but were noted by title on the contents page). The arrangement of the individual books and pamphlets in which Langley's poems originally appeared is given as an appendix.

Note (1994)

Every brushstroke changes the picture. If it's crimson it intensifies all the greens and there's the new problem in how to respond to that. The poem makes a start and you read what you've written, and from this and from what you half have in mind, the next bit comes. Sequence poems make the process visible. Many of the best poems I've seen over the past thirty years have been sequence poems. Don't talk to the driver. Not until some time afterwards. Crusoe standing thunderstruck, looking at the footprint, toes and heel, facing wide-reaching options. It might have been made by the devil deliberately to tell him something. Or by himself on some previous, now forgotten, occasion. Then the word 'toe' is close to 'token', 'sign', 'mark', even 'miracle'. It has connections with teaching, showing, indicating, having dignity and being worthy. Also, when walking through a bright nave, the various shades of a foot come from different sides, all at once, to join under the footfall. Ideas, etymology, experience. 'Juan Fernandez' ran ahead of me well, feeling fit, keeping me surprised. It has stayed in front over the years, and isn't exhausted yet. I don't write many poems, so each one has to be able to keep running, faster than I can, for as long as possible. I can't do without the autobiographical experiences, whatever happens to them in the subsequent process, however they got together in the first place. The sharpening of their distinctiveness, and the sense of their being separate from each other, and from me, lift, as Wallace Stevens said, 'the loneliness of thinking'. The shocks of fear and joy that specific moments seem to carry, for me, are often what matters most. 'What is really here.' 'Nooks and ends.' A flycatcher. A nest in the hammerbeams. Ford Madox Brown in August 1855 painting in the fields at Hendon, determining to 'make a little picture of it', while the clouds alter the light and the farmer carries away the corn Brown had chosen for his subject. He decided, eventually, it was better not to 'dream of possession'. But entertaining the dream is trying for more than a 'mock-up of consciousness'. It calls for testing all available strategies. 'Not things, but seeing things.' That could involve for instance finding out again, this time, what would happen if rhyme came back in to do a lot of the running. So, six years later, 'Mariana'.

R.F. Langley

The act of finding
What will suffice

Wallace Stevens

Twelve Poems

(1994)

Man Jack

For Jane Williams & Bob Walker

So Jack's your man, Jack is your man in things.
And he must come along, and he must stay
close, be quick and right, your little cousin
Jack, a step ahead, deep in the hedge, on
edge, a kiss a rim, at pinch, in place, turn
face and tip a brim, each inch of him, the
folded leaf, the important straw. What for.
He's slippery and hot. He slides in blood.
Those lies he tells you, running alongside.
To and fro he ducks, and miserably
clicks and puckers up, and in his rage he
won't speak out, or only half. He's short. He's
dim. He'll clench his jaw. He's more than you can
take. He'll drop it all across the road and
spit and go. Over the years you'll have to
learn to pull him in and let him know. You'll
say, 'Today we'll have that, now, those other
apples. So. Oh, but you'll fetch them like I
seem to think I dreamed you did, and they'll be
like they always should have been, in action,
apples in the apples, apples' apples,
through and through.' And then you'll see what he can
do. He'll fetch them in and put them roughly
in a row. The scent will almost be a presence
in the room. 'Oh, but it hurt,' he'll say, 'to
pick across the stones, the different stones.
So many different pains.' Oh Jack. You
hick. You grig. You hob. You Tom, and what not,

with your moans! Your bones are rubber. Get back
out and do it all again. For all the
world an ape! For all the world Tom poke, Tom
tickle and Tom joke! Go back and carry
logs into the hall. And wait with lifted
finger till the eave drops fall. Your task. The
jewel discovered by the monkey in
the shine. Fetch that, and make it much, and mine.
Sometimes it's best if I forget to ask.
An errand boy with nothing up his sleeve,
who stops to listen to the rigmarole
to find he cannot leave without he's bought
the dog. Time out of mind. Just bring
what you can find. Apples. Twigs. Icicles.
Pigs. The owl that watches as we try a
phonecall from the isolated box. Jane's
disembodied voice. The owl that hears her
words. The moon that thinks about her baby.
Jack in the moon. Jane in Jill. The baby
coming sure and soon and bright and staring
at the apples which keep still. The owl had
no idea. More knew Tom fool. The apples
shine in everybody's eyes. Tom speaks
inside his cheeks. The moon talks from inside
his belly. The isolation sighs to think
of motherhood. We hear Jane's tiny words,
as does the owl, astonished, listening
in the roadside wood. Jack gleeks inside
his only box of tricks for what has come.
All thumbs, he Tibs his Tom. It's apples and
it's owls. He bobs and chops and nips until
it's Jill engaged in paradise, with the

enchanted pips. Just in the nick with
only magic left. No use at all to
look at him as if he were a jug. As
if he were. A twig is evidently
a love bouquet. The apples are a gift.
The spellbound owl sits round as such
upon a shelf. Its silence cries out loud
as if you touched it on a wound. It is
embarrassed and delighted with what Jack
has found. And that it had, itself, the wit
required to secretly decipher it.
Until there is a sudden dip into
a silence in the silence, and the owl
has turned his head away and, frightened, stepped
off on his long legs into air, into
an emptiness, left by Jack who is not
there. He's gone too far. Though nothing drops, there's
nothing caught. The twig is two. The gleek is
three. There'd be a mournival in the four
but no one's counting any more. It stops.
The apple is not fire. And yellow is
not sweet. Jane's voice from miles away is just
a speck and almost lost, but yet it is
distinctly Jane, uninfluenced by the moon
she has not seen, the roadside where she has
not been, the owl who thought to pick a peck,
the apples she will never eat. The Jane
who cannot tell us yet the baby's name.
And, undeclared like that, it wins the game.

Mariana

And, looking out, she might
have said, 'We could have all
of this,' and would have meant
the serious ivy
on the thirteen trunks, the
ochre field behind, soothed
passage of the cars, slight
pressure of the sparrow's
chirps – just what the old glass
gently tested, bending,
she would have meant, and not
a dream ascending.

And, looking in, she might
have seen the altering
cream of unemphatic
light across the bevel
of the ceiling's beam, and,
shaken by the flare of
quiet wings around the
room as martins hovered
at the guttering, she
might have soon settled for
these things, without the need
for certainties elsewhere.

So, 'Please,' she would have said.
'We could,' she would have said,
and 'Maybe,' mildly. Then,
selling out, buying in,
the drawling light and the
quiet squall of martins'
wings again, again, she
might have soon discerned her
self, seeing them. Not things,
but seeing things. And with
such care, it would be like
being shown what was not there.

It was the old glass cooled
the colours and transposed
them in a different key. It
chastened most of what the
sparrow said, and made an
affilatura of
the tree. She would have known
the consolation that
it gave, and smiled to see
the unthought-of tricks she
needed, and the sort of
liar she was, or might soon be.

As things came in, and as
they spread and sprayed, she could
have tilted up her face
in the soft fuss they made,
encouraging the cheat
with shivering lashes,
tremulo, fermo, wide
or tight, intending
to confuse her sight until,
perhaps, she dared to make
a try – to find her own
cupid in her own eye.

To such a scene, amongst
such possibilities –
the downright, matter of
fact determination
of ivy on the trees,
wriggling queerly under
the examination
of the glass, the steady
sunlit room, fluttered by
each martin as it made
its pass – to all of this
she might have deftly given

a lash, until there were
sequins in the air and
surreptitious cupids
glancing everywhere. They
pricked their wings. Their arrows
spun away with thinnest
silver chirruping. They
were miraculous, picked
by her to be beyond
belief – believing them –
the lie she told to throw
the truth into relief.

Into the pure relief
of ordinary light.
But now she must have all
of this, compelled to see
by possibility
just what the glass finds real
enough to bend, jolted
by tilting shadows that
the martins send, seized by
the amorini, who,
being unreal, demand
her head for what they steal.

The Upshot

We leave unachieved in the
summer dusk. There was no
need for you rather than me.
Here is the unalterable truth.
Outside the open door peculiar
bugbears adopt the dark, then Kate
passes across. Next to nothing
depends on her coming in.

Here are the eight absurd captains
whether they are seen or not. Here
their sixteen certain shadows on
the whitewashed wall. Here a hundred
ruffles, grey and jade, coolly laid.
My hands and feet are already lost
in this country, with the immediate
sadness which no one has to believe.

The captains have not moved though
earlier the peep of day had staked
everything on the ear and shoulder
of just one of them. But soon he was
smoothly snubbed like the other seven.
Now the individual is unimportant but
eight determined men stand penniless,
never a glance, in the silver evening.

The odd outside matter that twirled
around all day in the blebs of gold
needs thinking about. Gorgeous. Like
looking in a pool. My chickens drill
and strut, piping my own particulars.
I won't leave it empty. I save a cricket
on a hassock – anything that moves, lies,
quirks, shrugs, can make a face and wink.

The drollery of that fiery ear. A hunch
I held sparkling for some hours then
sacked with the real severity inherent
in the air of this place. My patent
excitement is poppycock which needed
volunteers. There's a chance Kate saw
more by not coming in, but I only peer
at the backs of the eight deaf heads.

In here we're less lit from the sky. We
count our twenty four and are in jeopardy.
It is my sleeve creaking or a faraway
kittiwake, baffled by woods, brushing
my ear with a jeweller's fingers – which
leave what? Next to nothing. So little
and so icy that the floor flattens in the
afterglow and a multitude stands up.

They stand up but don't go. All ready,
not started. Full stretch in their rigid
heads. Now, when I need it, I'm so close
to emptiness. But I know too much about
each of those eight fixed faces. Unless
you ask about the eyes. You do. Here's
the opening for the hundred tricks Kate
took by walking across, not looking in.

We leave unachieved in the
summer dusk. There are no
maps of moonlight. Things
stand further off. We find
peace in the room and don't
ask what won't be answered.
We don't know what we see, so
there is more here. More. Here.

The Ecstasy Inventories

We slow out and curve
then the deep lawlike
structures loom and bob
through. We sway up, shut
down and open, coolly, each
small hour. Quiet. Then
quieter still. When thin
rims of rose and powder-blue
start slightly and a marble
runs down a chute.

The beach is stocked with one cobble
and another until you have to be
particular. Which are these tiny kickshaws
or tricky grenades on the old mud peppered
for ten thousand years. I've been noticing
how they needed low light and stale eyes
to catch such humble cajolery, all along,
hatching with soft pops into articulate
habits or costumes or clothes in a great
press: the broad, the heavy, the paragon,
her most scarlet gowns.

A blackamoor spurs by. The picture
of an Moore on horseback. Who
next? In a wink, in a pinked
petticoat, in a waistcoat set
with spots like pinks, in one
worked with eyes, she ambles
the lanes. An Moore on
horseback. The picture
of an Moore on horseback.
St Jerome. Mr Coke's mother.
Worked with eyes. Blue eyes.

The warm sun in some June. This June.
Both Junes. Take now and make a then.
A room. A roomy workshop. Elderflowers.
Forget the scent. Here is a carpenter,
singing. It is a hymn. Never mind
the scent, forget the difficult
bushes. Here is the hymn
from this contented man,
who cuts a shield upon a mantelpiece,
good humoured and intelligent, but the
cool, slow-motion, vanilla, bombs, ribboning . . .

The cuffs, collar and bedclothes
have lace on them. The lace can be
mentioned as strips with discs
or wheels, as sunbursts
of logical straps, rays, pips,
split pods or crooked stars, as
much as counting and nice
as a pocketbook with every
species, in flight, at rest,
in colour. These inroads let
me understand, and mark
sharply. Over what? Over
brilliant quietness. The path
ends in the shadow of trees.
In the trees I can't see the tiny
passerines all about in the
sparkling confusion. Or
her cheeks. Or her chin.

Follow the come on to the regular
heart, where we shall read a long
page. O my friend! The thrilled
ripples and cicalas and the dark
where the path and the story
beat through! Boreas did love her,
here, illustriously, with cicalas
and rippling. I can hear some
Hippocentaur's lips take hold
of grass with the resilience of
grass and that old ripping sound.

Silver moon; thatch; owl on the gable
and twelve silver instruments on the desk
for surgery. Silver moon on the desk.
Twelve silver instruments constellate
behind clouds. Ready for the straw
bird in the house of feathers. Mild
fingers set twelve silver straws on
the shining wood. There is a soft
interjection, stroboscopic starlight
and the powers realign. In another
box there are two gold rings.

No virtuoso in the glade. Just
heaviness in the darkened boughs
and twigs akimbo say I must
leave my father, try to go, months
ago. Dancing Mickey tossed
his chin and both his arms so
that the yellow gloves shot
glittering out and curved
sadly away. Gone, in a rigmarole
of little evil grass. Come
to pass.

White hedonism cut on blue
intelligence and laced
with silver anxiety. Bravo.
It braces milady's cortical
layer to take what could
have been trauma but now snugs
a bee in a comfort. While ants
silkily fidget and moderate
men press on, juddering,
grinning, being temperate
because of the price of beer.

Folds pack away; there is no crash.
Amongst the carnivorous thus and
thus and thus come two grey eyes
as you think, 'Is it a comma's wings
make such a silky noise?' So the
grogram, the paragon, snarl. So
fighting for their ranges the
wolves forget the deer. Or they
would hunt them out. Peace.
Famine. In the border zones
the butterflies are all eyes.

In heaven, where they don't
refurnish often, there will
still be an old white bodice
cut on blue and two lost
roses. Sure, in Walpolelane
there is a whirlwind of old
clothes. You would have thought.
Until a closer look saw each
was not vexed but folded
in unexpected readiness
in the press of the storm.

Juan Fernandez

1

As we slowly exploit the opportunities
between the jug and the earth, sky, men
and divinities, somewhere along the hold
the spring has, the ring gaining the ear
as it is picked up, the print on the bar,
the head shakes, shakes in a rainbow nexus,
shakes to see the old marks so very plain,
shakes the traps in reflection, rattles
the concentration into scrapping across
the frame, fluttering, mercurial, rabbits
vanish, turning everything into a large
form protecting the small ones, a spread
hand mothering doubts, as, now that
whoever that was has stamped past, they
wrinkle out, filling the hollow again.
And now is the water as firm as a heel?
Back drops blue sky. Convenient steel.

2

Snug, close and whispering up a trade, we
peep abroad again to find the planets,
earth and stones still satisfyingly alike,
sanctioning a lot more familiar adventures,
though we absolutely don't explain that
impression. Toes. Tokens. Miracles. Don't
you fret. We are gently rocking again.
Which makes it wonderful to rediscover
the silky wet print and deliberately fit
the foot back in it. I stood like one
thunderstruck. It was too big. By a great
deal too big. It was not mine. Loose my
cattle. Demolish my bower and tent. Wear
very quiet clothes. I've left school and
nobody cares about my motives now. Nothing
is clearer and more simple than a row of
rabbits caught outright in common light.

3

It is a common experience to come upon a
pale, glittering house set far back across
a meadow. It is certainly inside you. Down
along hours of mumbling 'Hello', and for
the attention of nettles in their darkest
green listening uniform, whose steadiness
miracles your ridiculous modern feet. In
its nimble way the lease suggests you can
project yourself, be big as the ancestors,
in this tangy, tart-taking, distinguished
deal. 'It's a light touch,' he shouts back,
'that will cause a great burning!' To which
the response has to be a firm shake of the
head or a slight widening of the eyes. Then
he's hurrying up, laughing, with his silly
reassurance that 'It's only you!' and
another blue funk is absolutely everywhere.

4

The print over the bar is the order of release
and it's away home again, ransomed deep into
a second time, deep into a pale blue, silky
head, billowing, billowing, a mite of quick
silver rousing in the threads. It bites. The
smell of meths just opens slightly round the
lamps. The unexpected colours stare. The crowd
is wholly intent. A fluttering. A blaze. Then
justice on justice as prodigious striding
shadows come to shut under this foot that I
am putting carefully down. The self is felt,
as standing, fired, inside the diamond. He
elucidates every projection and teaches what
was hidden in the heart. Of what is really
here. Of nooks. Of ends. Of wrinkling leaves.
The sparrows to the trees outside. So quietly.
The leaves just open up and let them come.

And all along the breastworks the dominators lean
and sneer. And I sneak and look up and match snarl
with snarl. It has always been in me to know how
they snarl. And I've done it before as a child and
a dreamer. The power is in dark, steady beams. I
sneak and snarl. But now there's a tiny request. A
cautious sip which might be surprising. It is hair
brown, or even lavender. It is a faint roughness
that stops. A flickering that hops to a deep nest
where the old frame burst its black heart. And she
twinkles in there with a beakful of wriggling legs.
During the last stages of the struggle, like this,
and only through a medium of dim instruments, came
baby fact. A particularly gentle thrill. She wore
silvery bluegrey. Sparkling. Startling. And the
brooding self with all its vanity disappears. You
forget how it is. Then. Whizz. And a perfect catch.

6

Could be that, when the carpenter stops to look
up, just as he straightens, his first idea will
be to see what he's been chewing. And the late
afternoon will open into a stunning exhibition
of honey and pepper. The awkward handle of the
saw. Its shadow on the bench. The shadows of his
fingers next to it. Curling. The separate worm
holes in the wood. Nothing seems so alive as the
tense silence of this picture. A new assessment
has released everything into uninhabited islands.
Into a final order. No. No. No. Now style alone
replies tamarisk on the dunes. Curling. I am
indicated by a star. And a footnote. I have been
shot through. Some sort of dancer must have been
here. But command is taken now by those tiny
expert birds who perch, and glow, and whizz
and pick the pepper out of the closing air.

Matthew Glover

To start with throve heavy forest
this district, on its marl
thick blue marl

a wood, preformal

no stream showed downhill
no hill rose up
but like a seasurface
this tract waited
for a mark, for a –
they would call it

    navel

    which someone did
    and from which came
    great benefit: as they cut it
    out of the trees

    they had it
    first time here

        shape, clearcut
        opens the four directions
        cardinal points in the previous wrack
        hollywrack alder bramble oak old
        dragon

        in good shape now for
        them to go to bed
        point their feet south

            if they wish

and the roof
opens
the fifth way
that is, heaven

meanwhile, and because they
watched the moon, over the clearing
they had an image for growth and decay
implying resurrection.

      the east edge of the parish now
      is a stream in a sandy ditch;

      a shelterbelt banks it:
      alder, willow, some bigger trees,

      and the scene here is,
      at the hedge corner,

      a fine, detailed bush, dead,
      a wicker cage now

      where three or more warblers
      hawk at the flies.

      and, as the light changes, they are soft
      brown or soft yellow with such restraint

      that their flanks
      shew like ice

      as they shift
      the small fizz

      of their flight
      breaks into

      your thoughts . . .

watching them is to see
the idea of a bird come

over into sight and sound,
momently, secretly, so

hard to see them in the air in
the bush there is no space

for implications: they have slender bills
and jet eyes; of colour

they have as much as the light gives,
not ever much beyond olive and white;

they keep themselves
within pure outlines.

In the midlands the village, everywhere
with its Open Field, system of which
little is known but
at its simplest two fields:
Westfield: Eastfield,
Northfield:
Southfield; each decade adding
towards the ultimate territorial limits but
all the time, sacred space, paradigm,
unfolding from the navel outward
to the line where villages will meet
or commons begin or
the colefield begin.

Enclosures in this parish cut up
the Open Fields round its centre
before 1758 and took the Commons

30 yrs later, fast, from the
declaration on the church door
to the Commissioners' meeting,
with maps and rules, at the 'Anchor',
15 days, one objector, one resident
undecided. From here we have,
minor changes only, the present fields,
squarish, five to ten acres, hedges
with quickthorn inset with elm,
spaced, bright willow by the waters.
Fox cover too, in odd corners, 'gorses',
Stonnall Gorse, Cock Heath Coppice, with
ruled borders; and the straighter roads
were laid now, 1800, by the 5th April:
wide verges where blackberry grows
and cow-parsley. Farmers moved out
into their new fields with red brick
Georgian or Victorian, fast as they could.
Here, though, is Mill Green: the stream
through the millpond, through the osier bed,
a small settlement at the boundary of parishes
because of the water. Here then
the lane is narrow, the older fields
wide water-meadows, the air rank, the
small crack willow.

the sharp fizz
of the wings

whose white lining
glints like signals

as they jump in
the basket of dark

brushwood, distracts,
like Matthew Glover,

resident, who would not
speak for or against.

All is lost
by such an arrangement

took a walk in the fields and
saw an old wood stile
taken away

all my life

a favourite spot
which it had occupied

the posts were overgrown
with ivy it seemed
akin to nature and
the spot where it stood
seemed taken on lease
for an undisturbed existence

all my life

my affections claim
a friendship
with such things
the small willow

the small crack
willow is dull

until the low
wind creams it

up with a purr
like bunches of

paper it blows
it purrs it purrs

Owning very little land
rated at eightpence
very little soil

maybe I did wish
to oppose the Bill

but I dared not do it
for fear I had missed . . .

A long time
I imagined

each square
five acres

I turned it
over

in my mind

no distractions.

The shapes seemed abstract
but handled well

at all speeds

were, in a way
pure, that is

admirably active, ingenious and bold
and operating on variables to effect
whatever transformations are permitted
by their definition.

as fair, you may say, as
citing the cycles of the moon.

But how
it shone!

used to, with the radiance
of delightful allegories!

Allegories. Some things were
full of fame; it will be long

ere their memory, their tales of it,
it might be a stile, or a willow
where tracks met all my life . . .

the moon, the lining of
the leaves

of the wings

Here
the light going
few notice the corner bush
is already an airy cage
where small birds flip
almost silently.

No tales about the willow-wren
please! What? Noise?

noise?

       he is too slight, almost
for one word

       he is
a bird for this moment and
the next

but no more

and his colours
excite no feelings, almost
no hint

       or half a hint

not enough to decide.

Saxon Landings

1

Here is of all the very this
is at last to keep the signals
lit or soon, they might, who knows
for sure the shore to either
hand so quickly in the haze. And
this could, once, so it has been
solid and level, hold on, then
here is inside your head laid out
in zones of shells and leaves like
you always hoped, not real, but
cool, it throws white light in
your face would you step out
under trees under tumbling trees
hold it still in both hands.

2

Through by the door, in the fright
of it's done, it's shot in a
click, though it's not light yet
the smells are sharp the bricks
don't blink, you blind as you
tell it this is action action
action and the treasure, heavy
silver, warm lids, mother table,
olives and cheese and bread and
possessiveness of a simple love
the whole zoned, beaded and scrolled
just gloats, it just gloats and
push it somewhere away into soft
loam and leave it afloat there.

3

Once they believed it but since it
is diction, the pipes in the wood
or limber vine and the bland
country where Bacchus and Pan
defeat Hercules. They lift him.
The drunk. Hush. Lay him down in
the sound of his name on the ground
of our home these are loan words we
never except as ledges of leaves of
shells this is keepsake and darling
and silver in moonlight is cold
twice cold, it throws white light
on your face you look blood
less in the porch's daze.

4

Your calm, my lady, has been
to have it your own, and known
hot to your ankles your knee
on the seat and talking windows
looking windows into arcady,
delectable, putting out white
poplar forming with your berry
mouth leaves or winter acorns
where your mood took listening
to there shall it suffice your
poet to have sung but this is
a very it cannot, slung on my
hips out my corner eye, rake
hell, orgies, waters, unlimited fury.

5

Save yourself stop this reflective you
can't think it sling it and run my
voice is quite shrill because while
you've been ships have beached, some
bird yelped, the face of a god looks
straight at you were eating off his
sacrilegious like a picnic his eyes
pop fish squeeze out his hair he really
rages lady! your chair spins his flashes
darken the windows his mane his mouth
is an open road under tormented forest
trees you walk gasping down his roaring
maw carrying your silver dish still
carrying you've been given a silver dish.

Arbor Low

White
arse
birds nip off stones which face
down. The birds tight on hip
fop and haptoe. The stones

dead. Sigh. There. But birds
burn off the tips of the fallen with
particular
flicker off
continuous stiffs down countless

once. A deepening hiss. Zig
with, zig
like
colour ripped off a just
after you hush like you

look inside at the big
still stones in the parcel of
now. But
a rude
fig a smart right at

some who come carrying deep
sighs to bring off the big
glamp onto all that comes
bubbling
through shining

reams off
the dark
bodies that rise in pale
apprehension. The birds fig
off like bits that snap at

the wrapping, unwrapping of greedy
to pass back to wives, to friends,
with open bags the tons of immovable
to be
alone then

they drive off with just a small
faraway
in the
glove compartment and bubbles like
someone the champagne had an

amazingly vivid but
little but little
bright
farts
of the birds.

The Long History of Heresy

Under the roar walls ride their
warriors and that unstoppable
young lord without a sword who

was a murderer. In all that fury
he sees at once. And nods. As
if he heard a sound, turned round

and found a bird in the court. Dun
pavement through a rush of coloured
slippers. While down along the quiet

waits our man, old nose, star
tooter, under a tree, leaning on
a heavy kill he won't know how to

use. Its polished edge bristles
with a thousand rays, steely, rosy,
blurry, sticky with a mix of saps. So

much consideration. Some folded
leaves. Some pierced. Others eaten
to the veins. The flies, in silhouette,

moving about the memoirs. So deep
into the book. Improbable fiction.
Old smears. But in a trice the young

lord found it easy to forget. The glass
cracked and a shower of coloured seconds
sprinkled away. Suddenly our man brushes

meal off his neck. Light agitation and
grasshoppers mix into more and more
stars   stars   stars   stars   stars.

Sneak drops touch leaves. They
wink. Flicker. And flicker. I
rush round to throw cotton-reels,

pin-cushions, short silver chains
into each bush. To play 'Gone' with
all the toys. To fit bobs into many

many sorry mouths. Won't we soon know
the whole shape of the lady? Our man
can only groan and twirl the blade so

that the constellations sail out to
settle into different shadows. Fingers.
Moths. Daintiness. Hopes and memories

play lips and blinks with blues and
pinks. Sometimes the softness of a
shower seems so shrewd that the foliage

is an inferno. Too many pats to be
married. Tickled to bits. But then again
the encouraging warmth of tonight with

coloured lights in the pub garden, over
the green, steadily seen. This bench
is built round the trunk. You might see

them on moonlit bushes, on the twigs, on
the night war was declared. Their eyes
both bright and full. After an hour I

worked out that the establishment was due
to a grip I had on it all coming from this
astral crimpling at the root of my nose.

Always, close to us, are one or two
motionless, big leaves. Then the
labyrinth. Dim groups and crumbling

lights which we collect and feed. But
the young lord's determination is such
that only ghosts are waiting at the

next intersection, only fancies power
the cloudy foliage. He is to be going
through, and out, smooth, untricked,

hitting infinity in a spick of fire.
Anything might be his sword. Each time
he passes through he finds his friends

have more and more about them, but he
smiles. Didn't he kill one of them
once? What the patient intends to mean

is irrelevant. Anything, as it moves,
might now and then stop to nest and
rest, arranging some shade and some

interest. But such organisation is just
the stop itself, no more, a footprint,
here, moving some trash, pressing it

to stay. But only an indian would know
of such places, want to keep a prayer
where a ghost took a breather. Our man

remembers a few, and smiles, pressing
a clenched fist into his heart. Anything,
but anything, is the young lord's word.

He's one who never dreams of possession.
He speaks and brightly rustles up some
suggestions of this evening on the small

screen of trees, the commotion of flash
and asterisk, but he is not referring to
any of this. 'Listen,' he says. He says

'Straight, white water.' And listening
becomes glistening. Lightning contentment.
Which our man sees as taking place against

some storm, a silence in the heavens,
inside some sort of a travelling pause,
where a mature lady steadily feeds a

baby. 'Listen,' he says. 'The Naughty
Boilers.' And our man roars with horrified
excitement as he chases a furiously

damaged sparrow which he dares not quite
touch. Then, 'Dainty Dish,' he says, at
last. And the whole canopy begins to

patter under a spray of hot urine until
our man staggers in the pandemonium and
slop to fall flat, quite passive, crying

desperately, but quietly. How was I so
willingly defeated? I was forced to give
over when I felt the big drops piercing

the foliage overhead. The warmth of the
uncut grass. In impossible furrows. In
tufts. Near green. Dove gray. An unusual

rosy pink in the unmade hay. I can make
nothing of lover's violet and the dark
long throws. Of muffled rubies. Nothing.

Nothing. When you're taking my breath away.

Blithing

The first of the ecstasy
singers screams soft scissors
open fans of leaves and a prim
little crack trims millions
of tendrils off all round
the space

Now, careful. The fern
carpet itches with pieces
of charcoal and bargaining
chips but the little grey
cock hoods bid after bid
over his thousand-stick
orange blink orange blink
orange

it tastes wise
and very dry
this little
decided kiss
till out of
selected non
drip shadows
walk the raisins
and nuts

I should think I will probably
have to come here again. On
one of those wayside tabernacles
you could read 'Illumined the
placid sea' and 'Unequivocally

aware that we were seated on
the shore. Nov. 17th.' and on
we went under the spray which
trancelike bloomed

Why else the signs saying 'Deeper
In' and the huge unsplit banana
leaves and the thin edges
of listening, entire, swimming
through clear water with open
eyes after the neat pink prawns

O you, O you he
this, she this
here, once, and
again and again
fieldgate. Such
shadowing

Come, opus one, or
little loaf in
the shape of a
found in the rain
of fired bits after
the stupendous silent
explosion, one piece
in the shape of a
girl

Rough Silk

So it best be away from home.
Some travel. Somewhere sour.
So there is there. Shrewd
issue. Not yet mine. The

same in time. Low time and
over-rolled by cloud enormously.
And others small. White squip
alongside as we come. And having

come we found it what we'd said
but just the notes of dreams, put
away. So here. We made it
do. Near the coast. Night

air. Which we knew did not
much care. Nor did the poplars,
flexing, nor the bats,
bitterly. Nor the old, cold

tabletop. What we drank stood
ready to go like the side of
a head. We kept on drinking.
Unbidden thoughts come sometimes

lustrous. Maybe this.
This garden. Was about
to be run for us. Well
now. And poplars pursed.

Poplars supposed so, gave us
up, rolled open like a bodice
sighing. 'Poplars,' they said.
And we agreed. We

smacked that. In rows of
standard authors. Poplars.
We kept on drinking, risked
some bats and closed some

shrubs like scissors. No
need now, no need at all, for
more than our well-bound
popular readiness. Drunk

and relaxed, yes,
and tumbling his
hands spread his peace
ful fingers slowly

opening, bringing his
loosely heels over
his heads slowly
together, yes, to

a pressed and an
interlaced ten
finger moon and
so husky. Such creamy

trash our stinging moon comes
through. Some local gods pop
homemade gunnery so briskly
that fuel fires right across

the foliage and now there's
rippling red agreement and
ginger stabs crackle accurately.
Hellfire. The central tingling. All

women and ambush. Classification
goes wishing up the glass. Streamy
rules. In a golden dear. After
all. Creamy dusk. Boppin' Flossy's

tresses in the creamy, starry
dusk. Quippy to the sweetening
core. Oh Flossy. Persuasive
Flossy. Now you're here knees

flood and I don't need to row.
The shelves on the edges I
can reach, and they will be
limpid, even when the main

point rattles uncontrollably
stubborn and humbling. I am
voyaging already at unsmeared
horizons right and left, out

of earshot. Nobody stayed to face
that musky bosom flapping with
pipistrelle and fighting screams.
They all threw in together and

their trinklements simultaneously
scattered into white water. I
quietly remember that lost
property and I keep just one

cheap brooch, a shell, set
sidewise in pewter curls.

The Gorgoneion

Once more the menace of the small
hours and of coming to light and of
each sharper complication. There was
a loosening which let much neglected
detail out of the dark. You can't look
away once it's started to move. This.
Must. And so must this. In bitter little
frills and hitches. About in a suspicious
twiddle are the tips of someone's ten
fingers which could, sometime, touch
mine. Something it is I would. I know
the sort of thing. A sorry moth. Sheet
web on copper pipes. I catch my whisper
that I won't be coming back. This still
increasing presence is for the last time.
Then the beginning of an immense grip.

If this is a crisis then I'll tap away
at it. Reflections cringe and scamper,
hover, then come back to where it hurt.
They bunch into description and find
some manners to be taken with. But if
you're smart enough to stop the spider
you'll see his fingerwork is not quite
mine, although the threads jig less once
settled in Euclidean space. There is a
certain silky insidious amusement as the
sun runs off brilliant free copies both
in filigree and queerly inflected on the
wall behind. Stuck here like a simpleton
you begin to smile, to suppose, to think
in terms of proof, until you are hooked
by it. Until you are sucked as a thumb.

You'd think at least the small, quiet
things could be decided. But if you are
content enough, and happy to sit down,
then all at once you're riddled by the
fast trick of the demon doubling his
shadow on your knee. Once here, he posed
himself in complete seriousness with
just one quick rub of his hands. On
display to believers everywhere. Crimson
eyes fixed in a dealer's stare. Hold it
there. Nobody move. This odd arrangement
of the crumbs and the letters rigid on
the packets. Sugar. Blazing. The whole
deck. Slammed. The anger of what can't
move itself at all. Every damned object
in this room is rapt. And boobytrapped.

There's someone here who says it's simple
as loving a muffin. Someone who pulls on
his conjuror's gloves and kids things softly
along. I can't say it's my way. He reaches
across the table in the glare and touches
one thing after another as if none of it
mattered. I can't say if I've still got
teeth or ears. That must have been one hell
of an explosion! But all I recall is a
patter of warm applause. I wasn't there
ready to be born, and I didn't stand up
at the end, shrugging. I have to keep on
trying again, cracking my knuckles, snapping
my fingers, hoping to get them to feel
like mine. With hands like these I can
only be confident if I trump every time.

Hands shaking. Because none of this
will ever happen again. Old hands.
The backs of them. Professional
wrinkles. And still I don't know
their tricks. Nothing I want settles
anything. Put them down on the table
and let them rip. The wandering cards
twist and jumble through them. Light
from the streetlamp outside collects
some leaves and the lattice to assemble
them, briefly, here, on this wall where
all is forgotten as the mime at least
comes true, giving some sort of select
account of what things do. It's a strange
relief to transform your fretting into
the silent coiling of a phantom dragon.

Spellbound, now. By the slow movement of
the jewels settling into the heart of the hoard.
I doubt if I'll ever walk back to the village.
Sure cards come so smoothly that it's cruel.
Are there only things to endure? But the
cobwebs adjust to the sleepy lapse with
blue sputters or a flick of what might
once have been wings. A flash off the terror
of hopeless love. They started and glanced
at each other. The cavern is filled with
muttering. It is the witty little histories
of insects making some sort of sense of
mud, hair and dirt, until the thunder is
over, and warm rain begins to fall in this
stillness. Then a hand is laid down and
another turns itself upward to be clasped.

from
Collected Poems

(2000)

Jack's Pigeon

The coffee bowl called Part of Poland bursts
on the kitchen tiles like twenty thousand
souls. It means that much. By the betting shop,
Ophelia, the pigeon squab, thuds to
the gutter in convulsions, gaping for
forty thousand brothers. So much is such.
Jack leans on the wall. He says it's true or
not; decides that right on nine is time for
the blue bee to come to the senna bush,
what hope was ever for a bowl so round,
so complete, in an afternoon's best light,
and even where the pigeon went, after
she finished whispering goodnight. Meanwhile,
a screw or two of bloody paper towel
and one dead fledgling fallen from its nest
lie on Sweet Lady Street, and sharp white shards
of Arcopal, swept up with fluff and bits
of breadcrust, do for charitable prayers.
The bee came early. Must have done. It jumped
the gun. Jill and the children hadn't come.

How hard things are. Jack sips his vinegar
and sniffs the sour dregs in each bottle in
the skip. Some, as he dumps them, jump back with
a shout of 'Crack!' He tests wrapping paper
and finds crocodiles. The bird stretched up its
head and nodded, opening its beak. It
tried to speak. I hope it's dead. Bystanders
glanced, then neatly changed the name of every
street. Once this was Heaven's Hill, but now the
clever devils nudge each other on the
pavement by the betting shop. Jill hurried
the children off their feet. Jack stood and shook.
He thought it clenched and maybe moved itself
an inch. No more. Not much. He couldn't bring
himself to touch. And then he too had gone.
He's just another one who saw, the man
who stopped outside the door, then shrugged, and checked
his scratchcard, and moved on. Nothing about
the yellow senna flowers when we get home.
No Jack. No bee. We leave it well alone.

Jack built himself a house to hide in and
take stock. This is his property in France.
First, in the middle of the table at
midday, the bowl. Firm, he would say, as rock.
The perfect circle on the solid block.
Second, somewhere, there is an empty sack.
Third, a particular angry dormouse,
in the corner of a broken shutter,
waiting a chance to run, before the owl
can get her. The kick of the hind legs of
his cat, left on the top step of a prance.
The bark of other people's dogs, far off,
appropriately. Or a stranger's cough.
His cow's white eyelashes. Flies settled at
the roots of tails. What is it never fails?
Jack finds them, the young couple dressed in black,
and, sitting at the front, they both look up.
Her thin brown wrist twists her half open hand
to indicate the whole show overhead.
Rotating fingernails are painted red.

Who is the quiet guard with his elbow
braced against the pillar, thinking his thoughts
close to the stone? He is hard to make out
and easy for shadows to take away.
Half gone in *la nef lumineuse et rose.*
A scarlet cardinal, Jack rather hoped.
A tired cyclist in a vermilion
anorak. Could anyone ever know?
Sit down awhile. Jill reads the posy in
her ring and then she smiles. The farmer owns
old cockerels which peck dirt. But he is
standing where he feels the swallows' wings flirt
past him as they cut through the shed to reach
the sunlit yard, bringing a distant blue
into the comfortable gold. How much
can all this hold? To lie and eat. To kill
and worry. To toss and milk and kiss and
marry. To wake. To keep. To sow. Jack meets
me and we go to see what we must do.
The bird has turned round once, and now it's still.

There's no more to be done. No more to be done.
And what there was, was what we didn't do.
It needed two of us to move as one,
to shake hands with a hand that's shaking, if
tint were to be tant, and breaking making.
Now, on the terrace, huddled in my chair,
we start to mend a bird that isn't there,
fanning out feathers that had never grown
with clever fingers that are not our own;
stroking the lilac into the dove grey,
hearing the croodle that she couldn't say.
Night wind gives a cool hoot in the neck of
Jack's beer bottle, open on the table.
Triggered by this, the dormouse shoots along
the sill, illuminated well enough
for us to see her safely drop down through
the wriggling of the walnut tree to find
some parings of the fruit we ate today,
set out on the white concrete, under the
full presentation of the Milky Way.

Poor Moth

Reasons run out and we are
ready to play backgammon
once again. Come on, I say.
I know when I am being
watched. Even in the washroom
here's a window left unlatched
and various small monsters
have nipped softly in to take
up key positions amongst
sunny patches on the walls.
Look at the little angels.
Chits of demons. Fools and spies.
Look at the conclusive way
in which their detail lies. One
touch would be catastrophe
or a whisper to the wise.
This mop is in the corner,
the hand towel folded to this
size. So everything is trim
in its replies. And three small
moths have six small eyes. Oh to
be merry with my friends! Oh
to be playing with only
matchsticks for the prize! Maybe
a lion would bleat, were it to
have goat's feet. Jack looks up a
chimaera in the book. He
flips casually through to
find it under 'J'. But it's
cross-referenced to where we
are today. To the sun stripes
on the green gloss paint, the types
of grass moth, who they're working
for, and why they put this mop

behind this door. The problem
in its purest form. There's Jack.
A figure I imagine
I can see far off in a
dark library. He's deep in
the reference section, where
a distant desk lamp bends his
shadow round the corner of
the stack. The librarian
has forgotten him. His arm
is lifted to the shelf. He's
fingering the spine of an
encyclopaedia which
he's just put back. It told him
something terrible about
himself. The revelation
prickled, and his fear struck me
as I was turning off this
tap. The echoes slip into
a quiet gap. I notice
I am breathing. Carefully.
I have to understand how
it was settled that the moths
came here. Signed up and waiting
with their wings wrapped tight. And ticked
twice. A double tick to make
it clear they have been checked and
are correct. The sun moves half
an inch. The journey will be
finished by tonight. Nothing
will matter in a million
years. I wonder if I gave
one frantic gesture it would
uncover all the complex
information, suddenly
silvery, riffling quickly
through the well-thumbed pages of

this ordinary place? Is
it a washroom in this case?
But here we are, and now. So
further instructions folded
in the wings are sure to seem
merely pernickety. I
know that if I blow on them,
they'll flicker open and be
right. Sunbeams stretch. Suspicions
glint. The questions narrow in
a more aggressive squint. This
is the arrangement on the
hot wall at midday. They stick
to it. What could I want that
they would give away? Rigid
with scorn, each cocks a minute
snook. However close I come
they won't exchange a look. They're
coded, rolled up thin, sealed with
a tweak, and then delivered
on the triangles of light
so accurately that you'd
swear that everyone had heard
a great voice speak. Jack staggers
between tables with the shock.
He leans so heavily on
a chair he makes it squeak. He
is tensed up and ready in
the gloom, no longer able
to confirm that this is the
reading room. In the silence
he gabbles explanations
in his head, spells words backwards
or counts syllables in lines
he could have said. He's aware
that I am mocking him, and
responds by taking trouble

with this idiot, the chair,
propping another silly
proof on four old puns in pairs.
Surely there must be something
that it's like to be a moth?
Some unique loveliness? To
believe in this would be as
if he creamed together runs
of interlacing ripples
being played on different
guitars. Transparent membranes
spread and glisten round his wrists.
His shoulderblades are braced as
he insists. Because he wants
a star, he rataplans his
drum, pressing it hard against
his abdomen. This could be
the best occasion for us
both to take a gamble on
the evening air. Jack nods.
I dry my hands. It is a
serious affair. We stare
at one another from a
distance, considering the
difficulties that are there.
We need to choose the roads and
hostelries. We must decide
exactly what the smell of
coffee is. Our picnic will
be nearer to the coast. The
food we have to share will be
scrupulously presented
on the grass, as a welcome
for any monster who might
pass. I expect a moth to
flutter round the tablecloth.

The Night Piece

The lock up is on. Someone
cackles in the goose house
at the policy of monsters.
In the white kitchen I
jump up and rub my hands.
Never a footprint out
there on the moonlit snow.
Then I squint. Then I know.
Plenty of small manifestos
wherever the blue mice go.

Mop and mow. Someone blows his
nose at the goose on duty.
I wade into the next gloomy
instalment, hissing through
my teeth, searching in straw
and strategy and all that
endless so and so. Then
the repartee runs briskly
round the rafters. I switch off
my torch and watch the eyes glow.

I must make a gate in case there's
a message. I make it twice.
The goose lies in wait, strict
with hate, in the barn. She
tots up her bill and the mice
shew two incisors each.
Certain truths cramp the corner
of the windowsill, but Jupiter
reflects on the pane. Or a
wandering lamp down the lane.

Try the outside tap, but
don't hold your breath.
The thick air has gone thin.
Listen to me. Little
is certain. A mouse springs
a trap. I massage bare skin as
goose pimples begin.
The narrower the gap
between curtains, the more
vivid the point of the pin.

Cronos collars the old yew
with iron. The darkest tree
sets out stars round its head.
The goose is the only Roman
left. She parades up and down
engrossed by the tip of her beak.
Why on earth should a sentry
seem so bereft? If I said
'Bo!' every dead inch of
the yard would squeak.

Exactly. The latch snaps. Now
the traveller could pass, but he's
pleased to lean on his cudgel.
Metal hugs the exhausted wood.
The port tastes of the vessel.
The bag stinks of cheese. The goose
stops, frozen, at the end of
her shadow. Stand and deliver.
The mice are delirious as they
wrestle in the crackling grass.

The Barber's Beard

By Wednesday afternoon the wind has dropped
and there can be a shakedown. When I tap
the stems, black seeds jump off onto the snow
and fix themselves, so Jack says, according
to the disposition of the stars. It's
Alexander's dust, he says. It smells of
myrrh. It's Macedonian parsley and
also, he says, the surface of fresh snow
is more like fur. Each seed is caught in this
soft stillness as a small orb in its place,
tilting its face, and very tenderly
presented to the air. Now we expect
some music in the distance, from a house
which once was there.

              Yes, Crustyfoot, we guess,
has made it to Piepowder Fair, and so
we know that Scipio will soon be back
from Africa. He'll blow in from the north
on Scandinavian gales. He'll be disguised
as a big thrush, dancing and flapping in
the cold bathroom and shouting out, 'I'm home!
I'm home!' Home in the roofless ruin up
the track, where Jack's map says 'Old Hall' and all
the drifts are deep and new. So, in the glow,
thorn by thorn, another diagram of
the strategy of last year's brambles has
been drawn.

I stop and stand where paths cross on
a Wednesday afternoon. Where else am I?
Somewhere there is a story being told.
I recognise Jack's voice that's quietly
telling it, as he describes how a man
is standing underneath a tree. How he
can see the standing of the man. He says
he feels his coat is comfortable and that
his shoes are doing well. The comfort of
his coat and what is watertight. He sees
that the ash is carrying its bunches
of ripe keys. The tree's carrying, and the
carrying of the keys.

                The amazement
of Scipio in his shaving mirror.
Show me his shivering. Show me his quick
smile that flutters out about the edges,
and spreads as wide as the blue backs of what
must be a flock of fieldfares, suddenly
flashing round the lime-green branches of bright
winter hedges, and he . . . who ? . . we . . . at once
smell soap, and unexpectedly catch sight
of an awkward little grin attempting
to take flight, avoiding the circle of
reflected light. The only witness's
white face, frozen as he realises
that it's up to him. The him it's up to,
disabled by his role in last night's dream
and terrified that I am Hannibal.

Dustyfoot arrested in a blaze of
alibis, blinking like an idiot
and hinting he's a friend of Jupiter.

Are you all right? Is he all right? Here is
the list of all the dead elms in the ditch.
If you need to check the details you will
find the same old worn-out wormholes under
any scab of bark, and nothing about
the arrangements to tell you which is which.

Well then. Good morning Jack. Don't slip away.
Just for a moment there I thought you'd gone
while I was shaving you. Please look on me
as if I were your barber, concealing
my irritation that you're late today
by gossiping along in this sing-song,
hiding the gist of what I have to say
in brisker chatter.

                Suppose the felties
were to pick out every berry, laughing
mysteriously, 'Tchak, tchak!' That Jack himself
were the piper, and his son stole sweets. Which
silly little theft, for all the shouting,
turned out to be, not just a merry lark,
but princely, attended in the dark by
cherubim. Believe it. That the bodies
of the elephants rolled over on the
bitter snow. That schedules barked. That a freak
tide exposed the northern wall as they stormed
across the lagoon at Cartagena.

Then it would seem that all the answers could
be ticked. As if the nouns, detected in
the depths, began to glimmer deeper yet
beneath the things, so all the secret eggs
grew wings and even Hercules was sure
his debts would settle out of court at last.
Then keys could hang fast, waiting for a touch
in March from sleepy moonlight. Scuttling verbs
could trap elusive opportunities
among unlikely roots.

                                     But just as it
occurred to Jack that he might count the flock,
bird after bird displayed an ash-gray rump.
They've turned away and opened up.

                                            They are
about to go.

                           This is the moment when,
flummoxed to know what else is left to do,
Jack and the poet and the pronouns shrug,
take a breath each, and melt into the blue.

Tom Thumb

We should accept the obvious facts of physics.
The world is made entirely of particles in
fields of force. Of course. Tell it to Jack. Except it
doesn't seem to be enough tonight. Not because
he's had his supper and the upper regions are
cerulean, as they have been each evening
since the rain. Nor just because it's nine pm and
this is when, each evening since we came, the fifty
swifts, as passionately excited as any
particles in a forcefield, are about to end
their vesper flight by escalating with thin shrieks
to such a height that my poor sight won't see them go.
Though I imagine instantly what it might be
to separate and, sleeping, drift so far beyond
discovery that any flicker which is left
signs with a scribble underneath the galaxy.

My job, preparing for the dinner, was to peel
the shrimps. Decapitate them first, then, stripping off
the legs, pinch out, if they were females, all their black
and yellow eggs. And Jack, as usual, was not
at hand to help me do the damage, manage not
to curse out loud. We both know why. Distracted by
a resonating croak, he watched a heron stroke
unhurried to the south-east, past a rosy cloud
to the full moon. And then involved himself in how
the gnats above the chimney shared their worrying

together, working out their troubles in a crowd.
They must have done that every summer, all my life.
Jack says he never saw them doing it till now.
He makes a few impromptu jumping movements on
the lawn – his imitation of agitation
in swarms of innocent shrimps and prawns. And slow blood
slithers through my listening. This is the whine that
my poor ear can never hear, from the gnats high up
above the cowl. It's Jack's droll warning. Always there's
someone mourning. Always an invisible owl,
one of whose party tricks is knowing how to scowl.

Look Jack. I'm well aware what's going on when your
forefinger and your thumb reach out like that to give
the air a tweak, a twist, to tune in to the sound
you say I missed. What then? So maybe I pick up
a hum. Some fiddling from a belated fly that
landed unobtrusively on a hidden stem.
It's there. A minute elbow jiggling. Nothing more.
Doubtless this is the very moment when it saw
that you had marked *appassionato* in your score.

Between the nails of my forefinger and my thumb
I nipped the heads, pulled off the bushy whiskers and
bright pips of eyes. The shocked expressions came away.
But these were not actors. They were not wearing masks.
There was no second face beneath to recognise.
Jack didn't breathe. The midges seethed, where, I dare say,

there was an updraught through the flue, a warm one, though
without a fire. But he was staring higher at
the final suggestions of the swifts, rapidly
dashed off, carelessly punctuated with a run
of dots that flared, then melted immediately
into thin air. No doubt the lightning sketches of
the many different shapes of what he called despair.

Look Jack, again. Suppose that here we are in this
familiar room, and reaching out to shake hands
with our old shadow on the shiny knob of our
well-polished wardrobe door, to take out, once again,
the peculiar man we used to be before.
Can you pretend you need to have a photograph
of him in mind, to check we get exactly what
we think we'll find? Hello to last year's summer shirt.
The sleeves. Their flap and dangle. Halloo, halloo to
the ferocious gestures of the swifts, the flash and
chop, the quick contortion to escape at a new
angle, into a new glide. And every one I
know, because each is at once beyond compare. Each
action and its brilliant illustration simply
coincide. This is the fly, so tightly fitted
in its place I feel its savage elbows piston
in and out, though all it does is carefully wash
its face. I remember how, back in the bedroom,
I had to struggle with the shirt. But who buttoned
it so neatly? Then, in the garden, who reached out
so sweetly through the stinging nettles to disturb
the stem? Who delicately shook it so he could
identify the fly? What virtuoso played
that quiet capriccio? It was not Jack, nor I.

This thick-wit is my thumb. I cannot miss him for
he fetches wood, digs pignuts and ties shoe laces.
Three hundred motor units in him act as one.
He snaps open carapaces, pulls out white meat
and pinches off the faces. Sometimes he softens
the spiccato, smooths the document, signs my name.
Spirits obey. How goes the day? Oh, easily,
so long as you don't ask the way. I promised to
be here for dinner, come what may. For goodness' sake
you Jack, be dumb. Inevitable detail on
the moon, grows to perfection in a silent bed.
The heron spoke, and meant precisely what it said.
Gnats twinkle, and Jack glances down another list
of items due to be removed from the display.
Swifts vanish in full flight, against the changing of
the decorations from pale lemon to pearl gray.

Stop taking stock, and listen. They have briefly left
their voices, sharpened to incisive single points.
The screams of fifty little demons on a spree,
going home excitedly. Meanwhile, of course, the
heavens mutter, and the shopkeeper has put up
his safety shutter. Fireworks crackle for the end
of festival. Jack is jumping. The rhythm of
the gnats is hot. Up there, the chimney pot is squat.
We have finished eating supper. Stare at the cowl,
if you're so certain that the hunch must be an owl.

The Face of It

(2007)

Cakes and Ale

This bit again. You know it.
It's the sequence in the bar
on an outer planet. You
see piecemeal through the ruddy
strobes and smoke. You must be by
the door, and going through the
motions, brushing off the rain.
Their backs are to you. Hunchbacks.
Some of them wear metal. Fanged
pauldrons, bizarre combs frizz up

against the strip light further
in. Barbarians. Or a
culture in elaborate
decline. Flagrant. Capricious.
You ought to recognise which
tribe. Those red plush tippets. An
occasional glimmer of
a souveraigne collar, if
you're right. Some Gothic warriors.
Braggarde and dangerous. They

have not yet looked round. One turns
to speak. And now you see his
beak and thin, uncurling tongue.
The customers are monsters.
The customers are monsters.
From deeper down somewhere, some
instruments like soft trombones
start blowing a blue hockett.
The customers are monsters.
They have not seen you yet, but,

when they do, they'll love you limb
from limb. Meanwhile they face the
wonderful barmaid, who is
all their mothers still. She gains
her glory nobly tugging
every polished handle in
the middle of her rosy,
pumping heart. They need their nips
of sack and sugar poured by
this real lady, level to

the lips of their own greedy
brimmers. Now she'll look up and
see that you have come, in your
perversity, her erstwhile
son, through the tempest, on the
last night when it could be done,
to the back door, for, once more,
a sop, a sip. Only your
haggard stare can win her. No
secret wink gets you this drink.

Nor the guts to shove you to
the front, as you hold out your
father's empty bag. This bit.
Again. The hockett stops. The
strobes lock rigid at the top
of nightmare. Then a dragon
starts to swivel in his chair.
The barmaid's million hands
close on this one pump handle
and become a simple pair.

Cook Ting

Circumstances analogous
to life and death, house cleaning or
clutter. Dante or an old shirt.
It's there to cut, but not to chop.
Between the knuckle-bones it's soft
as butter. Or you picked a leaf
off the road. What is it when it
reaches the sea? The gulls are a
white flap over sprats in the foam.
Call it an episode when they
tumble together to make it
one. The cliff is history. You
throw yourself in where the fish are
thickest. Take hold of a word and
turn it on. Tourbillion. A
blade is so sharp it can dance round
the joint. Silvery energies
argue the point. The carcase of
an ox flops open. Shall we leave
it at that? Some of the cliff calves
flat. The rest ducks, and runs like a
rat. Look about and wipe the knife.
But there's more, there's more. Rubbing it
out will prove there's no nub of the
matter. There are too many eyes
for your own eyes to catch in the
scatter. Twelve blank sheets of paper
hung up on a string. The joy of
perpetual bicker. Your seat
at the open door. The shutters
banged back. A dark acrobat who
somersaults through to rob a few
of the glittering company.
Is there a wife for a Viking?
A pair of socks in a poem?
Beetles and sticks in a box? Bright
bait. Bright bait. You notice what has

gone into the picture. Bite it.
It can't be expected to wait.

Experiment with a Hand Lens

The clown under
cover. Among
a lot less. Aghast

at much more. A
set of tucked legs,
curled up from

before. His mother's
bug. Her summer's
boy. A bead

she polished first
to put deliberately
last. Her lonely

coal. Kick start.
Heart prick. Fire
crumb. Come close

in focus. Here you
are. The cavern fits
the wren. Lenticular.

This is her son. Her
pearl in the pout. The
merry meal in her

floury mouth. And
so and so. Amen.
But ahoy you young

lout! Not so far!
Not so fast! You
can never tell when,

with that hole in you.
Nothing is less than
particular.

Sixpence a Day

The sea bulges or licks.
Cool as a lemonade.
A gull rides with its two
red feet, dib dab, beneath,
doing appropriate kicks.

So easily can the
low sun rearrange some
pegs, making another
countenance with its legs.
It switches hips, turns on

a toe. Marram shoves its
stems through silica and
an unidentified
spider starts to chew his
gloves. Now here he is, cream

spots on cinnamon. His
camouflage first becomes
his normal wardrobe, then –
Voilà! He's ablaze with
all his badges! Handsome

patches double on his
abdomen. You see the
sense of this, compared with
the mad quarrels in the
mix of flints. Bunch or run,

whatever he does is
excellently done. Gems
will be known and numbered
in the movement of the
secretary's watch. You

rip so you can match. A
nib makes flourishes with
an emphatic scratch. Where
nothing bothered any
more, draught boils a cobweb.

Forgotten by the world,
odd glossy bits blow round,
hang out, shake up. As keen
as mustard every seed
spits on his neaf. There seems

to be no limit to
the amount of life it
would be good to have, just
fingering the thickness
of a leaf. So what if

there are really no grand
narratives? Electric
peaseblossom flutters in
the surf on autumn nights.
Your rapier can still

spear the eel. It can pick
off this particular
caterpillar with a
flick. Your brain finds much to
amuse it in a bush.

You're the best friend of a
naturalist who hugged
himself, expecting it
to be a bear. Stand back.
Give it a chance to growl,

if it is there. The gull
glows. Dusk adjusts its grey
to that. Pit pat. There must
be huge commotion when
you touch shocks of grass. Eight

eyes. Brightest the golden
pair. A clink of chitin
as eight knees slightly clench.
This heartbeat underneath
this cardiac mark, like

a soft pulsation in
a trench. It creaks in the
thicket. Come quick! The room
is full of them, as big
as birds! The great mounsieurs

in white neckties and with
their wings as floppy as
a melancholic's hat.
They hood and wink until
they eventually

clip the little ticket
which is shivering in
the muscle of your cheek.
Don't be dismayed. It's nine
o'clock. Lay all the stuff

you have collected on
the mat. Count the score. Do
the job slowly. Do it
well. Colour them in. Both
flick and flack. Maroon. Brown.

Ivory black. Once you've
got started, most of the
males will stop their flap to
settle down together
round the female on the

bell. O Peter Quince, it's
not knavery at all!
Cool as a lemonade.
The convenient place.
Just as you said before.

Still Life with Wineglass

A wineglass of water on
the windowsill where it will
catch the light. Now be quiet
while I think. And groan. And blink.

I am anxious about the
wineglass. It's an expert at
staying awake. How can it
ever close its eyes? It's too
good a defence against an
easy sleep under the trees.

The wineglass stands fast in a
gale of sunlight, where there is
one undamaged thistle seed
caught on its rim, moving its
long filaments through blue to
orange, slowly exploring
the glorious furniture.

Old Harry has opened that
bundle again. Oh well. Tuck
up your golden sleeves. Fetch out
the white gloves. We'll go right through
the thistle seeds till we find
Jenny.

The finch's mother
told him about teasels. He
consults them daily with fierce
resignation. His findings,
however, fluff out and cream
off, catching the drift.

                    Mum was
the word, but she did give a
nod. So they sidled up close,
put a foot on its neck and
kiss, kiss; kiss, kiss. Sometimes they
stopped pecking to watch what they
could not follow. Parachutes
whispering away

                    Milk and
magenta. A gob of the
cotton, torn from the button,
thrown into despair. So there's
nothing remains of what we
see? Does it? Does it? Tumbled
about in the air?

                    We speak
from out there and we keep things
alive. The wineglass reminds
me of wading birds, when their
beaks meet their beaks as they feed
on a mirror of mud and
mark 'Here' as a point in the
water that's deep in the sky.

Fetch me a folding chair. Set
it up by the south door. This
is etiquette. I am the
ticket collector. Nothing
comes in but thistledown which
scarcely touches the floor and
was never supposed to pay.

New pennies. Spun into the
droning paternoster. How
close Jenny rose to the top.
Then turned back, and you lost her.

Each bubble considered the
rest as it chose its place. Out
in the morning everything
settled, before I could look.
Down centre is a tomb or
shrine. The sun is shining on
the corner of a panel
set into its side. It's all
paid on the nail. None of it
is mine. Way off, and running
strongly through the hazy, slate
blue sky, that must be rosy
Mercury, bent on a quest.

He did choose the third sister.
Jenny wasn't there. Recent
incidents are never seen
in the crystal ball. Only
a procession of distant
people, passing below a
ruined wall, brightly lit, but
microscopically small.

Soft pappus strings out like a
search party. It's looking for
the concealed figure of a
god. Whoever dropped him in
the clump of weeds forgot him,
so they could seek him in the
sacred hunt. Remember how
the wineglass put its foot down,
chip-chop, happy to be home.

Next. Invent a religious
uncle. He was the one who
taught you elocution when
you lived in the forest. Give
me the details. I want your
whole story clear in my mind.
Rabbits are kindling in their
burrows. Tomorrow Harry
will meet Nuncle just as you
described him. They will sit down
together in the sun and
puff at the dandelion.

A bumper. Little fingers
that were hidden flicked the dice.
The cunning rascals counted
on convincing you these were
the lucky accidents of
a busy day, set, at the
end of it, in solid ice.

The window. The wineglass. A
yew tree inside it, upside
down, far away and very
distinct. A cautious chaffinch
sits tight through the shift of the
consonants. The needles are
green. The bird knows it is pink.

No Great Shakes

Outside, the cones in the pines
are rows of turbines set into
the wind. But, inside, the mind
expects a blow.

Outside, each cone screws into
the wind by a twist of its
scales, up to its head. In here,
there is no thread.

Outside, each bit of twirling
pollen has the best shape for
the flow through the vanes of the
cone. Inside – none.

Outside, the twitchy stems of
grasses make quick snatches in
the air that passes. Others,
stiffer, with a

down-wind bluster, bounce the dust
till time enough for clustered
flowers to catch it. Here, the
mind can't match it.

I cannot tell. Get thee back
into deaf John's dark house. The
draught is trapped and whipped about
the wrist and strapped

so the cold fist warms somewhat
the fingers curling on the
palm. Four worn Jacks turn churlish
in the shaking

hand, grinding uneven teeth.
The same star still burns westward
from the pole. Cock all, I say.
Inside blown out

and topsides down. The clown's own
knuckles are the bones he's thrown.

After the Funeral

In the Ceramic Gallery. No train
till half past five. Yellow.

No amber. A hornet
would be something from another poem,
eager for nectar. We

fleer with yellow leaves. A
row of white bowls that make
mouths at it, months of it,
moon after moon. Colder
and rimmed with copper. In

the Ceramic Gallery, the yellow
October plane tree leaves in Gordon Square.
Nothing slabbered about Pauline's death. Some
details will rustle about or hump it
and call it a sixpenny jug. Think it
as leaves. Think it as bowls. It's a question

of leaves at the top of
their swell, which speak out in
a screed round the scope of
themselves, to die down in
the bowl. Stop. So that they
settle. Or stump up at
once. A hornet could bring
a formidable hum
to the poem. It's the
right time of year. There were
none at the Hampstead Free
Hospital. Nor here. Give

some mind to an empty dish. How, in the
Ceramic Gallery, metal lips fit.
Her passport photograph looks like the moon
in a tight woollen hat. She had given

her money away. Her
stare will say nothing of
that. I forget what is
left of the leaves. But it's
a knuckle keeps rapping
the bowl, so that it rings.
So that it rings and rings.

Depending on the Weather

The hurry to bite that runs over the spare
text, with his head high, with his bulging eyes. He
swerves with the weave, expecting his next success.
Premise:– the beetle believes that he knows what
the wasp is thinking. The beetle believes he
knows what the wasp is thinking of him, the green
beetle, what she sees he might mean, his needles
winking and the wicked cut of his jaws. The
beetle believes he knows what the wasp thinks the
beetle is thinking. About them both. All their
embroidery. His nip. His stitch. The set of
grapples in his grin. The rich twist of his you.
His green me. Two to embrace. Then the toils we
intended to trace. The last clasp. About how
clever to run through what needs must be done, to
be stitched up as them, as the beetle and wasp,
woven deep in and ready to work. But what
we remember, both, as anyone should, is
this shock of this buzz of these silvery wings.

The classic malevolence of the evil
fairy, or your own ill-treatment of the poor.
She passed by the door, speaking nothing. Then she
instantly returned with a like look, and in
the same silence departed. The new wheat-cake
I was chewing fell from my mouth. Myself in
a trembling. Myself off my stool, sewed in a
stocking. Stuck in my fit. I believe the old
widow knew well enough what went right to my
heart. What I ought with my cake. For the sake of
a silent rebuke. My neighbour, the witch, who
is after my cookies. Eye on me, as if
she were Atropos. Green as a beetle that
studies to bite through these golden curls. The twirls
of a wasp round a hot pocket of sand, as
if it were checking its property, combing
out honey. The kingdom of spin and snip. A
bobbing goblin. The hank and the quill of our
hungry fate. Escape that. We both think we will.

Imagine the beetle imagining the
wasp imagining what would be involved in
keeping a diary. I should have risked more. Done
nothing. Taken half, maybe. Never the whole
bake. But, it's a fact, no peas would then grow in
the field. They were unable to make butter,
or cheese. And that was it. A fly – always the
same fly? In summer weather it would shuttle
through the glints and darkness looming in her room.
Far too familiar, they said. Doubtless a
part of her repertoire. Some point of view, some
plenitude and cogency. Really? Nonplussed
on the glass, it knocks against the white outside.
It taps. His angry finger nail. Tap, tap. Some
privy agony? Eleven women, all
acquitted, and, it seemed to me, believing
nothing of the witchery! He sat up straight
as if the sky were resting on his head. The
wasp reads on. The beetle rips up what is read.

The beetle believes that you are watching it.
It lifts its chin, looks at you, and gets ready
to unsheathe its wings. The fascination of
a magician is ever by the eye and
to the heart. Mine aches. Dread hunts my ground as a
tiger beetle, reeves my quiet as a wasp.
I learn their manners and disguise myself as
them. But their movements figure out themselves. They
never choke on cake. It's a mistake to wish
that they could speak. They pass on this and that. Most
of this kind do take to the air at once, not
saying a word. And he cheerfully greeted
the more sensational testimony, with
the remark that he knew of no law against
flying. Staggered, they went out into the day.
Blind. Reeling with freedom. Who cares what they thought
that they thought that they thought? All such repertoires
are put to bed. The blanket design was an
old one, easy to pick out, worn to a thread.

Blues for Titania

The beetle runs into the future. He takes
to his heels in an action so frantic its
flicker seems to possess the slowness of deep
water. He has been green. He will be so yet.
His memory ripples emeralds. The wasp
takes it easy. She unpicks her fabric of
yellow and black, which slips from her fingers to
land in the past, loop-holed, lacy, tossed off on
the wing. The beetle is needled right through on
one string. He peels a strip as he packs a shelf.
He is thrilling the grass, and whatever it
means, it is radiantly green like himself. Thus
he will invest again and again in that
same flashy suit. The wasp has forgotten her
costume, but proves herself wise to the ways of
the sun, which are pat on her back. She drops a
curtsy, blows a kiss, and somersaults over
the beetle's attack. Lost moments swill round in
the shallows, until they can stick there and stack.

The beetle swears it's a set-up job. Follow
your mouth. Swallow tomorrow. Borrow and bet.
Rivet your eyes on the road, and do what you
said. You run through the beetles you have been, and
insist there are more of the same up ahead.
The wasp says goodbye to those she has never
met. She swirls down to just touch the track, so that
she definitely indicates her shadow,
a generous fellow, who has come on his
own, to join in. He's an item. And now he's
close kin. She gives him a hug. Then that's her in
mid-air and she's left him. He's a scoundrel, who
dodges about and grows dim. Neglected. The
necklace has snapped. Scramble for beads. Some of them
still roll and sparkle, prickling the gorse and the
stamens of the bittersweet. This will be the
best place for muttering nonsense. We could meet
anywhere in the wood. Tired in the hawthorn
brake. Tricked by the thick vegetation. Gutted.

A snatch at the clasp and a curse as our prayers
scatter. One of them comes to a stop by a
dazzling white stone. Others tag darker places.
So be it. Snipe lie near small pools, to hide in
their glare. Purple orchids are smuts in the dusk.
A wasp is humming as it investigates
the gravelly foreground, where no gods squat, but
someone pictured an overturned goblet. The
stub of a tree with a kingfisher on it.
Cybele carefully holds up a quince. Now
specialist theatres are opening all
along the hedge. Sparrows adopt passionate
poses in each of them. Detail is so sharp
and so minute that the total form suggests
infinity. Everything. Wincing. Oh, but
thereby, it seems to me, there is infinite
loneliness. Such tons of shingle. If I find
my feet in it, I will walk up and down and
sing, that they shall hear that I am not afraid.

The beetle straightens his jacket to confirm
an initial conception. After all there
are not many cores. The car doors slam behind
his shoulders and he pulls away into the
best, fast synthesis that there is, blazing down
the mid-line, the Roman Street, his heart in his
horn. The wasps and moths and feathers are riff-raff
off the verge. Stuff for his buffet. And isn't
Isis Demeter? No mysteries in here.
It's me, hands on the wheel, and capable of
brilliant wristy brushwork, if I rouse out
my conceit across the blur of foliage.
But. Who knows what monsters were revered by the
Egyptians? We must not boast or palter. Don't
rush the sense, or stagger if it's true. Ask me
not what. The duke has dined. Three layers of the
lapis, mixed with white lead. The last translucent
glaze, and no golden scumble. Cool and intense.
Guaranteed to be the bluest of the blue.

My Moth: My Song

It goes on. Hawk moths stammer in front of
the red valerian. These words, floated
in the silence, by myself, hover close
to my thoughts. The thoughts themselves almost were
words. I think they were. I think they did. How
close is close? What colour were the moths?
There was some orange on them, and the words
were white as water. Sometimes they referred
to orange. It is difficult to say,
for instance, what it is like to hold a
field mouse in your hand. It is exactly
brown, is it? But other peoples' words come
yammering about. You have to clutch your
own, inside your hand, where something seems to
prickle like water. You make decisions.
You don't experience them. Metaphors
are only other mice. This morning there
were other butterflies. Green hairstreaks. Two
kinds of swallow-tails, flat out in hot sun.
Linnaeus bedevilled them with Homer.
A battle filled with butterflies. No red
thorax, so he said, means that these are Greeks.
Achivi. Pectore incruento.
Pat as a kiss, one settles, unnoticed,
on the rim of Nestor's chariot. It
flicks open to the page that you looked for.
Pectus maculis sanguineis. These
are Trojans who have wounded Machaon.
And Nestor tapped his horses with his whip.
Pick up our surgeon, Machaon, and drive
him to the hollow ships. Papilio
machaon. The red valerian is
a city. But it's hard to character
the whelk and drift of waves. Their eyebrows flash
metallic green. Those hairstreaks. Sometimes a
shape will follow you all day, through thickets,
disturbing the names, old indications,

the sort of education where the wit
of man is hard put to it to devise
more names. Callophrys. Beautiful eyebrows
in the bramble. Rubus. Hairstreak. Hawkmoth.
Macroglossum. Big tongues in the bedstraw.
Stellatarum. Starry, starry things. You
can be hooked all day on a dab of song.
Suddenly, in the shadow of a street,
a symbol is a face held out to you,
and close enough to have immediate
significance. I will think a little
promise for you. I will wrap your cap of
ferret-skin inside your wolf pelt. I will
dump them in the tamarisk bush, till I
come back, when tonight is young, around the
corner of the not so far away, to
find, held out to me, as I expected,
waiting to be tasted, certain spoils to
make it worth my while to uncoil my tongue.

Cash Point

Took a turn or
two across a plot
of May, to where
he saw wild thyme,
some clustered oxlips,
bunches of riviniana
violets

And, the way Adam
put it, their bodies seemed
incorporate with their
names. Cobwebs, sticky
on cut fingers. Tongues
caught up in the sweet
lexemes.

So, speaking leaves, he
said, 'Commend me to
this Mistress Squash, your
mother. Drive me together
all you can gather. The
stars can't be so far
away.'

Bring me that fellow called
Hay. Uncork a bottle of
smoke. Help the old lady
out of the bush. Hee
haw, when the cart has
passed and straws still glint
on some snags in the hedge.

Close your eyes and make
a mum with your mouth
shut. Just so. Now
look. The stanza is a
born dancer, out on
the green. Tongs and
bones in your good ear.

The notation is numinous.
Some patient gentleman with
the beak of an ibis is
writing it up, in case
any honey leaks from
a bee's thigh, or a hip
verb.

Bosky. The occult
semiosis of the forest.
*A l'ombra d'un bel
faggio,* where you dip
into syllables and
emerge stringing
pearls.

What had you in mind?
Red sienna? The fur
of a lappet? The purpling
tips of its wings? Or
this little chap, nodding,
perhaps, and wringing
his hands?

With your last twitch you can
point at the letters that make up
the spell. Too late to explain.
You are trained to assume
the soft applause of the Latin,
levis and *labi*, as you ask for
a wind to ripple the carpet.

Freeze and scream. You ragged
devil! He erupts in a bray and
glares with what might be
recognition. Asshead. Dolt.
Blunderer. O monstrous! O
Thisbe! Only thine! Only
a ninny!

But we are not on
stage, so that might be
the magus, Agrippa Von
Nettesheim, approaching
the hole in the wall,
with nothing to suggest we
should have his number.

Take a map. Park the car.
Undo your napkin in the
moonlight under the Duke's
Oak. Sort it. Pace it out. You
don't need ribbons on your
pumps. Just a note on the key
signs and an almanack.

'What it means
is not what it
refers to,' grumbled
Flute, rubbing the
stubble of his
orange-tawny
beard.

Kiss the rubric or the prayer.
Kiss your stipend till its
corners chink. Kiss the taste
of a freckle, or what the cow
slopped into the rough-cast.
Kiss lime. Kiss hair. Whatever
you think is not my lips.

Shadows cascade
down bales on
wagons which pass
away under trees,
and I swear that
they are fluent
enough.

Touchstone

Aquinas was wrong.
Science and religion are
not continuous. Thus:
the late robin in the
dark garden. A gift,

a lock, a wedge, an
order or a wistfulness.
A real bird in actual
space. And matter
constitutes the laws

allowing notes from a
perch on the line-post.
The head cocks, which seems
astute. Then the further
limits of our being plunge

back across the forty feet
into the hedge. You can recall
the flutter in your empty
ear. The bustle of the feathers
in your ear. Their brief mandamus.

Augustine was right.
There was no 'before'. The world
set off with time, not into it.
Accompanied by dusk the
further phrases sing out

off the line-post, melodic,
desultory, sweet snatches at
masks, small personal cheers,
most of your education for
these years. This grass and dusty

hawthorn and this ten-o-clock
to float you home. Blue thistles
go to white. Magenta lychnis
blackens. A dragonfly is
allocated extra minutes to

astound the moths with vehement
flaunt-a-flaunt of possibilities. The
slight rustle of everything
immediate. Nothing here
is clandestine.

Descartes was wrong.
The decision to sing is
the first note of the song. It
discovers the bird there on
the line-post, as it is

already being sung. The
quick flexing of the legs is
unexpected. There is no
estimation of the hawthorn
and its forty feet away. White

thistles are what blinked.
Before it took a breath, the
robin was caught out in
what it saw, and what
it had to say. A touching

welladay? Not so. It was the
atoms of the August evening,
instantly genuine, distancing
themselves or perhaps
less torn apart.

Kepler was wrong to
talk of forces as if they
were things. Here they are
generated by the robin
which turns, now, to the north to

power a strict, ticking call in
that direction. The dragonfly
flays molecules along the hedge.
Nothing is mystic. The lure
is obvious and the bite is

a delight. What else is capable of
this spirit of alarm, together
with direct appraisal of the
autumn and the opportunities
of this very moment on the stock?

It has to be a material fool.
His warranty tempts me back
to see if I can find some record
of the magenta and the blue
which must be kept there.

Brute Conflict

It could be this. It could
be brute conflict. It could
be that I want to count
because I do not want
to count. The counter-wish
is wished to normalize
confusion. To desire.
To notice the absence
of the stars. Regretting
it. Glad that they have gone.
To calculate without
desires, so the pebbles
vanish when it comes to
calculation. Desire
for pebbles. The placid
images of shape and
weight. The cheerful pebbles.
The joy of having too
few fingers for the stars.
Abandon the trip to
the beach. Pebbles are so
much like pebbles that they
look back at you. Their gaze
rests upon you. You are
a disappointment to
yourself. What sort of a
laugh was that which you gave
to the night sky? Belief
is in this or that, but
you want horned poppies and
sums done without pictures.
You are quick to deny
your heart, but the leaves clasp
the stems and the seed pods
divert you with ribald
gestures. Four or five toys
remain on the table.

All small. None of them is
mechanical. Each has
come out of your secret
drawer. He could call down the
stars. He used anything
as an imprecation.
'You plate!' he swore. 'You lamp!
You towel!' But often
he saw a surge take up
the cobbles, jingle them,
then put them into place.
Often. Often. The same
rubbed round bodies of the
stones. Hit after hit. The
thorough hammering. No
cutlery. Brute conflict
and a restful nonsense.
Now five thousand starlings
no one ever counted
have settled in the reeds.

Skrymir's Glove

This morning in November in the bar
of the Angel there is an open fire.
I tell you this so you imagine it
as though the bar in the Angel were a
place that has been given to itself, full
of itself, filled with the things there are in
here, such as the fire. Not the words but the
flames. This is quite possible though you know
that what you have of it, its hum and pop,
could not be prior to the poem. You
don't take shelter in the darkness and the
cold of open countryside which, in the
morning, will turn out to be inside the
giant's glove. You sit down at a table
by the window where you can feel the flames,
take off your gloves, wait for Louise, who comes
through doors into such places, those given
to themselves. You still enjoy the way she
does, and here she is. Grey eyes. Black hair. Go
for the gloves. Fashioned by trolls, the food is
tied up in impenetrable iron.
The cat is stuck into the shape of sleep
and can't be levered off the floor. Your tongue
proves chocolate dust on cappuccino
froth. It's all as heavy and as hard as
that. But it holds good. There is some truth in
every bit of it. Louise can help, things
on her mind, her fingers lost around the
coffee cup. The good spectators will now
imagine someone facing her across
the table, where otherwise there would be
empty space. Someone is called to work on
a complete Louise, lever her off the
floor, fix her in iron, put her amongst
grey eyes, black hair, and seat her opposite.
That will be me, facing Louise, feeling
the fire inside the Angel bar, inside

the giant's glove, the window to my left.
I will arrive precisely when Louise
picks up her cup, touches the iron, wakes
the terrific cat, and both of us are
given to ourselves, together with trolls,
perhaps, and incredible November.

At Sotterley

Caravaggio raises Lazarus
on the Messina canvas
in Room Four, where they squiny
at the light that comes across
from behind Christ. Maybe they
think it is a snap of sun,
outside the cave, in March, in
Bethany.

          I walk, in March,
in fields, at Sotterley, and
look everywhere to see the
colour of the paint. Mars black,
iron oxide, chlorinated
copper phthalocyanine.
Green and grey and sepia
on the trunks of oaks. So this
is Martha's light, being left
to serve things as it can. The
work is in the kitchen.

                My
day was spent in walking through
the gardens at Notre Dame.
I saw his eyes were shining,
then I guessed that he had seen
someone behind me that he
came to meet. The glow of his
face is what I won't forget.

It's Lent. Unexpectedly
the oak trunks are caught cobalt
green.

          Martha is cooking and
nobody asked her what there
was to eat.

                    Ticket holders
like to think Room Four is the
dark cave where they get close to
actors they can recognize.
Back in Room One, this was the
man who grasped the table and
boggled with the shock. Which of
them is Caravaggio?
He and his friends are pulling
all the faces.

                    If I had
seen his wife and child before
I saw his happiness, his
face would not have struck me so.

A truth to content you. In
the shape of a jug. The jug
be my judge. I drink in it
so the cold water quenches
my rascal. I pull myself
together, gulping down the
lonely Martha. I grasp the
table. Here comes a long draught
of my small, stale, icy beer.

A family behind me
are whispering about the
colours, in a language I
don't recognize. They come from
a country whose pictures are
like none in this gallery.
None that I have ever seen.

These characters have been told
to pick the jug up off the
table as they would do if

they were picking up a jug.

I leave a perfect heel print
on a molehill. Green lips lick.
These touchy chemicals have
no self control.

        Warm it with
your ice-cold commentary.

I see the brushwork and I
read it back into the far,
well-swept corners of her floor,
the perspective of her path,
the Shrove-tide overcast she
glances at outside. One way
or another, if you are
a realist, you can do
no more.

        This is Emilia,
twelve months old and waving to
the Christ Child in the Titian.

The brush calls your attention
to the jaw, to both lips, to
the nostril, the eyelid and
the smooth bulge under the brow.
Six strokes of his post-Roman
manner, reciprocating
with what looked like the truth in
Sicily. Turn round and be
in Bethany. Slow down and,
lost in a stand of oaks, there
is a woman with a broom.

They do not know which way to
look, and miss the hands in the
air above them. That will be
Mary who dares not touch her
brother's head in case it costs
the love of love. They can't see
that, either. They twist into
the lighting from stage right. I
can't hear what they say, but now,
I guess, they shout for help from Sotterley.

The Bellini in San Giovanni Crisostomo

It's curfew, and I do my turn
around the valley, settling down
outposts of mine, the little, far-
flung castles, Roche this and Rocca
that. And 'Check,' I say, and 'Split,' and
'Cover up my fire.' I rouse my
sentinels under relict clouds,
happy with some altostratus
and a roll of rosy billows
processing off the peaks. I start
the spleenwort by the door, argue
small slips and petals which still snap
with love or hate although it is
so dark and late. I stipulate
which bits matter. White chips go in
grey spaces. But, gradually,
the old man's face becomes more than
it was. His profile is on the
sky above the mountains. Nor does
he look at me, but only at
his book. He veils his eye and sucks
his lip, as he considers what
is read. And so it starts to move.
The castles and the clouds and the
asplenium which I still make
out, splayed on the rock, are taking
their places in his head. He has
a mind for them. Together with
his library, his fig tree, the
ridge he sits on, the cinquefoil, the
other weeds in cracks, here he comes,
with screes and summits and summer
pastures in the gloaming at his
back. He edges forwards under
the perspective of the foreground
arch, between the pair of flanking
saints who are inside already,

standing on the marble floor. Each
thing he brings is sharp as a stone
which I discover as I shake
my shoe, and tip it out to hear
it click and patter to a stop.
There is no need to badger at
the garrison, trooping home for
supper. Recall your champions.
Inform the tower, the gable,
silk on a mitre, the paper
label tacked on the parapet,
that they can have one moment more
to be expensive. The moon picks
at the corner of the page. I
turn myself around to thank him,
the old man, the moon, Bellini,
hoping the next words he reads will
mention me, as someone waiting
in the nave, at twilight, here in
line fifty-seven, arrested
by green and rose. By rose and brown.

Birdwatching Poem

For Robert Stone

In the twigs, *contorta*, of the two trees
which the council has planted by the new
apartment block – eight waxwing, bibbed, masked and
crested. At first they were conclusive black
up there in silhouette, then they flourished
down in splendid grey and cinnamon, dashed
out with writs of zinc and red. The tails tipped
in gold. A hundred years ago, Mutzel
engraved them, posed in conifers and birch.
His foreground was the usual broken
branch. He sheathed this one in moss to show a
swampy place in Fenno-Scandia. Might
be witch-hair lichen. They came in Volume
Three, between the shrikes and thrushes. They don't
care where they come. Nor who is watching them.
March heat. The plastic gutters start to pop.
The birds drop to the cotoneaster.
Heads bob. A berry is held up in a
beak. They leave across the demolition
site. Now raise your hand if you think you saw
the grapes of Zeuxis. You've earned yourself an
All Day Breakfast at the café on the
disused airfield, sausages, mushrooms, beans
and bacon, toast, hash browns and two fried eggs.
There will be thirteen days of North Sea cold
and overcast. Next time, ten birds in white
tenacious light, clipped to that same bare tree,
all of their colours in unshakeable
positions. Say what you saw. Come to the
topic unrehearsed. The scratches in the
cave are nothing but a family of
snowy owls. The youth at Fayum forgot
he had big ears and that his mouth was still
somewhat tucked up as he imagined he
was dead. He felt how far it is. The nip

is in the small purse of his lip. It is
conclusive. Now it is flourishing in
his winter face. Now it has signed him. You
see that? And it is written so there is
nothing to translate. Mutzel, of course, saw
owls, and then a waxwing, holding a red
berry in its beak. Immediately
outside. Distance was there at once. There was
a disused airfield, people still working
in the café. Breakfast. Not far to seek.

Il Redentore

Eight hours out from Stansted then the
numbers can go handsome. The star
turn of eight between the six and
twelve. Unfluted columns. Whitewashed
walls. Corinthian acanthus
with volutes that spin up to trump
the tiers of leaves and clinch the horns
of abaci. In this calm light
complexity settles into
perfect focus. *Concinnitas.*
Correction hums. The length of smooth
grey architrave levels across
arrested foliage. Then comes
the creamy frieze, then, grey again,
the cornice. Hundreds of dentels
corrugate its strike. Loosed into
systems, other shadows of this
gentle afternoon lie upside
down on archivolts and cusps of
niches. Outside the clear glass of
the west door, the green canal puts
up a hand, and then another
further on, a second silver
hand, to show two corners of the
stone revetment, so that, from here
to here, there is *una certa
convenienza* in all the
body, *tutto bello.* Six is
to eight as eight is to twelve. You
step back into creamy heat and
your eyes go grey. Nine is to six
as six is to three. The ticket
for the vaporetto is where
it ought to be, tucked into this
top pocket. Eight is to four as
four is to two. *Valido.* The
day and hour. Both have come true. Your

tongue is held between your teeth. To
order and explore. Some certain
people stand where you can count on
finding them. A son you came to
meet is in the salizada,
by his shadow, rustling paper
as he checks the name that should be
by the bell. You had him timed for
half-past eight. It's twenty-five to
nine, and, *tutto bello*, here are
the hundred good hellos, ready
to say. More shadows follow files
of clouds that run straight off the coast
of Sussex. The warm ground raised them,
thermals which condensed in puffs to
be picked off by wind that took them
out to sea. Neurons move in the
mind, *psi, phi* and *omega*, Freud
said. Their quantities determine
their different directions. Well.
Tutto bello. And your eyes go
grey. A woman, dressed in black, moves
in the nave, diminutive. A
woman with white hair has entered
and is tracking east. The woman
carries stick and prayer book. Eros
binds, Freud says. The woman bears her
body stiff and black, bound in the
transparent air. She has strapped her
body to its backbone and she
keeps it up and going with a
stutter of short steps. Her aim is
to preserve the long walk up the
nave, and so she is a poet
and Palladio. Leg after
leg into the second pew. She
climbs in with her hundred legs and
bends her head. In retrospect I
can ignore the facts and see her
triumph there, a dark acanthus.

The Wall Tomb of Giacomo Surian

Magnificent eagles heave and
whap their wings on Bruni's tomb. On
Zanetti's is a *feston* where
an eagle thrashes. She spreads and
screams. In Santo Stefano, in
half-light from the door, two griffins
sit under the sarcophagus.

Tackle the right-hand one. Try some
account analysis and a
repertory grid. Tell him you
know what he intends. Pretend that
people can make choices. Treat him
as if he did. Ascribe to him
a moral sensibility.

Flatter him as if you nursed a
dangerous baby, as if you
were a widow with a sulky
cat. Invest him with panoply
which is appropriate. Curse him
for looking like a buzzard, with
no feathers on his armoured legs.

He heard you coming in, and ducked
and swung his head towards the door.
His beak is opening, and the
tongue inside lies flat. Nictating
membranes flicker up his eyes and
he will snap. The gimlet nostrils
have been drilled below a skinny
frill that serves him as a cere. And
he will snap. He will now lunge and
snap.

His talons are grabbling on
the modillion, which has three
crisped seed-pods cut on it, just as
it should. You twist his tail until
it pops into a tuft of flame.

Alongside him, a little fat
boy leans, inscrutable, against
the ear of the inscription plaque,
and he holds up a torch of *Hope*
or *Life.* Another time, he will
get round to some intentions for
himself.

Outside the door crouches
a woman. She holds a plastic
cup, and is the beggar on the
steps. I'm pretty sure that this is
her across the city, later
on today, outside the Billa
supermarket, with her mother,
both carrying two shopping bags.

Deep into these transactions with
myself I send for words that will
extend some eagles on the wind.

Achilles

One is seldom directed by way of
an indigo gate. A life is plunged in
colours, saturations, shades, tints, hues. One
screws one's eyes up. A mediaeval list
of inks confuses *fuscum pulverum*
with azure from the Mines of Solomon.
Who knows what perse is? Days lose themselves in
pandia omnia and dip away
between the pinks and blues. But then there is
alizarin which sometimes jumps from the
old leaves. And turquoise is a stone dropped near
the gamboge fence. Who did not notice those?

And shapes. The tree. It shows what one could call
constraint. It bursts through rocks in calluses
that clog into a lump with several
branches lunging out of it, one knot-hole
and a stump. The thing has corners to it,
pockets, ledges, wedges, all chocked in with
lichen on them, found out by the sun that
stabs down from the right, detecting olive
green.

In sixteen-thirty-three, when she was
twenty-five, on a creamy marble slab
in the south aisle, they drew Elizabeth
Havers. Did she have time to walk out past
a red house? Choose a brush? Paint a picket
white? Step on by? Turn round, look back, and shout
that she could see what it might mean? That that
was the place where she had been? She is a
whisper. Smoke and cream. What had she really
seen? She rolls her eyes and wears her shroud so
that it does not cover her lace cuff.

                                                    The
kylix has been cracked. The mend in it spoils
his cheek-piece and his mouth, but there is still
his eye, under the helmet's rim, as he
stabs her from the right. She reaches up to
touch his chin. BC. Four-sixty. Killing
Penthesileia. It is his last and
only chance to stare at her. He does so
and he falls in love. Or is it lust or
scorn? Furious concentration? Don't call
it blue. Not blue. The gate is indigo.

She is engraved on her stone slab. The aisle
window moves its print onto her face. It
stresses her lips, almost rubbed out, and the
scoring of her thick curls. Her tear-ducts. The
look she is giving to her left, which might
be sad because she is remembering
what? Ten minutes of after-glow, when white
campion seemed distilled against grey grass,
the poppy in the crop, alight, red for
itself, and she stood stupefied by that,
hoping the hero had not seen her yet.

If she had lived she would be sixty-five.
Sir Isaac Newton, in a dark room, pins
his paper, sets his prism twenty-two
feet off, and asks a friend, who has not thought
about the harmony of tones in sounds
and colours, if he will mark each hue at
its most brisk and full. If he can, also,
postulate, along the insensible
gradation, the edges of the seven.
Where blue ends. Where the violet begins.
The pencil in hand. The hand and pencil
are suddenly intensely indigo.

The gate is indigo, but when they give
directions people call it blue. To lose
the way is to remember something of
the stump. But can anyone be ready
for the moment when the dusk ignites the
poppy? Or accept that the spectral hand
is his? That it's he must keep the pencil
steady? Maybe everyone is dazzled
here by simultaneous death and love?

This morning in
the pool at

Lime Kiln Sluice
a heron wades and

his deliberations are
proposing ripples

which reflect on
him, run silver

collars up his
neck, chuckle his

chin, then thin to
sting the silence

where he points
his beak.

His round
and rigid eye.

Perhaps he knows
he is caressed.

Spoken Soon

Under superb
trees

wandering with a
sleepy wish

the shadow of my head
pre-empts me

full of its thought and
nonchalant, travelling

through trees. Thick
and fast examples

crowd the brink. I say
Enchanter's nightshade.

Yellow pimpernel.
Some smaller sort of

willow-herb. White. White
and magenta. Spick

and span and strawberry.
The sprangle of the tree.

The aspen as it takes possession
of the notebook. No-one

is buried in the sand. Enough.
I say a pile of logs.

Hornbeam and ash.
The bark almost intact,

polished or matt. Hot
in the glade. Bright

beetles nominate.
Thanasimus. Clytus.

The paragons run every way
in red and black and gold.

Enough, I say. Your
faces in the evening.

Spoke and spoon. Enough
the bowls of milk and

strawberries.
Mikael sleeping.

Joff with his lyre,
Naima recognizing me

across the water. My
bravery is carried down

a cart-road by the summer
breeze, on the dividing light,

at the direction of a cloud and
nonchalantly balancing her wave.

Uncollected Poems

(2008–2010)

You with Your Visions and Dreams

'So this will be "As if ",' the
script-girl said, helping to hand
out mediaeval costumes.
'As if,' the sound-crew nodded,
folding oilskins, pulling on
Icelandic sweaters. 'As if,'
the make-up man was sad to
say, blowing the snowflakes off
his broad-brimmed hat. At which a
great bird, flat-winged, high up, came
floating from behind the firs.
The way things were had kept it
hidden until then, but now
it circled round and we dropped
everything to watch. I thought,
'This is the way we make the
best movies here in Sweden.'

Aftermath

When you wake up it has been raining.
The angel holds up one forefinger,
levels the other at your chest.

Guess.

From the cold Adam, now,
and from the infant silent in the air,

> the droplets
> resting on the threads,

> the residue of breath
> left in your ear.

Guess from the spark
in the foliage.

> How did a shower sound to him,
> in the Jewellery Quarter?

> With his pronouns?

> They did a brisk trade
> in chrysoprase?

And this one, which you did not hear
last night, making itself with weather
that you slept through?

The angel saw it pass over.
Raised a finger.

Counting into the quiet.

Counting into the quiet.
Looking you in the eye.

The Best Piece of Sculpture in Perugia

Old vendettas, and no
details of them, or whose

heads were on the spikes. I
don't want to go down this

sad, steep street, sidestepping
vendors of handbags and

leather belts, only to
be remembering those

flagellants. But at the
bottom is a grass plot,

railings, a gate, unlocked.
Look. Bas-reliefs beside

the Oratory door.
Obedience shoulders

her yoke. She stoops her head,
lifts her left hand, steadies

the beam across her neck.
Behind her right cheek, the

shaft cocks out, pinching
a wriggle of her hair

against her jaw, blustered
in her gusty headdress,

so that it comes poking
from a rippling pouch of

cloth and hair. She looks up.
She opens her mouth. She

is listening to the
smooth pole coming through the

kicking hair and cloth, close
underneath her ear. She

tilts her head to feel the
disturbance eddy its

shadows against her face.
While, quick about, she is

bundling a tuck or two
of darkness where her right

hand catches up her cloak.
Her body rouses to

the surface, luminous
and streaming drapery.

What did I whip myself
with, tottering down the

Via dei Priori?
I spoke to no one. I

suppose that nobody
spoke to me. Probably

my envy sat at the
café tables. If so

I did not glance to see.
Now there is nothing on

spikes to hurry by. No
guilt in the voice or shame

in the eye. It is her
lovely marble, tawny

white, one rim of it scrazed
red, and many pearly

passages bruised with
dim mussel blue. She knows

that it behaves for her.
Her mouth is opening

but she is wondering
what I can find to say.

She is *Obedience.*
All of my audience.

In the Bowels of the Lower Cave

at Gargas, Abbé Breuil took photographs
of the engravings illuminated
from his left. He figured a fragment, the

forelegs of a horse, their feathering scored
dexterously on bright rock, unshadowed
by the hand using the burin. Twenty

years later the Easthams sensed the pressures
better done by a left hand, and moved their
lamp across. Then, manifest at once, less

deeply cut but a complete conception,
the whole horse stirred to take possession of
its legs. At Ekain, Bison Fourteen is

sane and sound, provided the source of light
is four feet from the surface, four feet from
the floor and twenty inches left of your

left ear. A flame. Regnant. Ducking. Wobbling.
In Magdalenian air. Stretch out to
burn a finger there. In the *Sanctuaire,*

sit, as five persons side by side could sit,
fitting their feet in the convenient
trough of stalagmite, and see the tumult

of the place resolve itself into three
bison nosing round the caricature
of a mournful human face. Position:

optimum. Gargas. Ekain. Trois-Frères. The
need to occupy the posture after
fourteen, fifteen, sixteen thousand years.

The need to be in the cave, to put your
modern body most exactly where you
know the Palaeolithic body was.

To reconstrue, outward from the nip of
shadow pecking at the graver's tip, to
wrist, to crank of elbow, up the angle

of the rays to the vital candle with
its wick, its twist of burning conifer,
ruby charcoal crumbling in a cup-shaped

scab of exfoliated limestone, held
aloft to right or left. As recovered
from the Shaft at Lascaux. This, that and thus.

Eight thirty. Tenth February. Frost smokes.
The rooks triumph, sneer and roar and throttle
in these polished copper branches. I hear

hooves trot on tarmac round the corner of
the lane. But it is water clucking past
inside this ditch. Water. A palatal

click. I took it as an echo from off
across the fields. Now this mistake fixes
the trick and trim of the nimble morning,

salutes the truth. Accuracy esteems
error. Both are so smart and tight they pitch
and play together, the drips of hidden

water and the sprightly hooves, here on the
side-road where dead fireweed muffles the verge
exactly where I am, halted by how

they speared the clay bear at Montespan, which
must be sympathetic magic. But huge
black bulls parade the Great Hall at Lascaux.

Bison superpose their haunches in the
Main Gallery. In symmetry. These
could be narratives or the totemic

ancestors making their arrangements at
the renewal of the world, emerging
from the Confusion of the Forms. The rooks

plane down to explore raw furrows for their
sacred food. Individuals voice their
scorn mixed now with some satisfaction. They

slaughtered birds but represented very
few. Why paint a sorcerer dancing when
you are a sorcerer and can dance? In

Western Europe, twice, they filled sections of
their lattice signs in solid violet.
Nothing comes trotting round the corner but

he is close alongside nonetheless, in
optimum position, the small bearded
horse at Niaux. I see him as he is.

Videlicet

Over the reed bed the marsh harriers
cavort for spring but far up and cruising
above them, a different bird, a glist,
a chequin in the fiery manganese
air. Their male, in his resentment, pitches
to reach it where, whiter and bigger than
he is, it pikes on the wind, levels on
five-fingered wings, black tips, carpal-patches,
which it holds fathomed for a moment then
slews and slents away into the blue glare.
No part of the sky-dance, of talons and
tumbling. It caught the drift, accepted it
and lifted on it into clarity,
to be the final shining fix out there.

As well as the obvious celandine
open on the bank in Edward's Lane, this
fribble of white flower is bittercress.
The single line of reflexed hairs along
the stem is typical for chickweed. I
meet my neighbour at the corner and we
speak about tomorrow's storm. Kirsten hoves
over her hedge to make a point. Background
details treaty deep into agreement,
each proposing this good morning and some
sharper recognition for itself. More
scrutiny of the south-facing bank. And
sudden Kirsten. And red dead nettle hides
four teeth of orange pollen in its hood.

Looking for something. Finding something else.
Any scribble is too easily made
into a face. First there is flamboyant
use of space. Then the suspicion of an
awkwardness. I had thought there were two pairs
of harriers. One of the four is not.
The graphics roll into a scuffle, bind
a confusion, wrestle themselves for a
discovery. The sky is opening
to the touch of an anomaly: the
other bird, full splay, stamped with black on both
its wrists. No fadge. No easy face. Kirsten,
intense, the very likeness of herself
against the sky. Emerging from the hedge.

A tap on the hat-brim. Snow is melting
from the branches of the poplars and the
impact of a drop suggests that I should
trap it, crisp, and take it home to brood on.
Keep it fresh for reference. More than the
blether of the usual to and fro.
I remember the white raptor as one
snapshot in the Album of Departures.
The stamens slip their cape and step to the
open door to warm themselves. As folklore.
Adam and Eve. I stare at them. They stare
at me. Kirsten is staring over the
hedge, above the hedge, across the hedge, braced
on her mark and expecting to vanish.

Rain wets the line of hairs. They conduct it
to the lower leaf-stalks. At the axils
these are cups with lips which catch the moisture
to absorb it or to spill it over
so they pass it on. The explanation
is itself a pleasure. But the stuff of
the hairs has gone, until the verb 'distil'
begins to prickle, liquid soaks back through
the letters, and again: that curious
strip of fur, the fourth bird sheering to the
north for the sub-arctic, the couple who
uncurl in the mouth of the flower, and
bittercress as bittercress while Kirsten
is sharing silence with the quickset twigs.

Practical Myth-Making

So then. Here, after all, is the old
earthquake, the old horse bolting as the
cyclist passes on his velocipede.
I was ready for exactly that.
The headlines in the paper on the
table next to my breakfast setting.
Nothing jumped. It came in quietly. It
was too simple to be much of a
person. But I could talk to it, have
words with it, the Declaration of
the War on France, while dust motes lazed it
through the kitchen. Could I not wheedle
with it? Make it a conversation?
I was always screwed up for the thump,
for things askew, slightly, teetering
along the top of the wall, slewing
black newsprint across my white linen.
A whiff of fox from the hot box hedge.
Woodsmoke from the almshouses. Catkins
and small crimson quiffs on the hazel.
Kiss every glimmer. Get things to glance
over here, pay me some heed, set their
caps at me. Was I not ready for
them? The proof of woodsmoke cut short
by the impossible stink of fox?
Speculations are sent wheeling through
the grass. The first light. Warm earth. Cold air.
Guttation. The drops are shaken and
tremble. I recognise these simple
people, who quake and bolt and spark and
float, and almost find themselves in what
they do, but look out, too, for me, so
we can wrangle. A legendary
creature stages its arrival in
this room, chooses the typeface, spreads
the white tablecloth, stands me in front
of it. Seventy years of this vague

foreboding. I stop to rock back on
my heels, to feel the iron of the
road. I become a target from all
angles. The catkins steady and take
aim, the buds deploy down twigs, open
cracks, push out minute bloody pistils.

The Bellman Confides in Her

Walking down into what seriously
affected his inner sympathies, what
was deep and complete, behind the dreamy
shimmer. Thick gamboge dragged across bistre.

The thousand repetitions of little
forms and what is bulking up amidst them.
The dark ox under the hedge suddenly
lollops into the headlights. The street which

twists left under the archway and flashes
two yellow windows. To nest in corners,
to hip the gables of the Genuine
Village. To take steps with Raw Sienna.

He has passed a thatched penthouse where they keep
their heavy roller, and an arbour where
two of them sit at a table, lamplit,
faces averted. White patch. A mob cap.

In the first version he has ignored them
and they him. He swings his bell and he trails
his stick, steady ahead into intense
love of Kent, Devonshire, the Apennines,

the phantasmagoria of mighty
sunsets. In glory the tree is topping
the cottage. In our humble doubt about
our present faculties its species is

unidentifiable. Later, in
the etching, with her hands again on the
table, she now looks up. Black eye-socket
and mouth. He looks down at her, so I guess

from a small alteration to the tilt
of his hat. It is at this time that those
windows glow, the tree sets out its palmate
leaves and spikes of pale horse-chestnut flowers.

And whoa! I smell them! There is a calf
with the oxen. Angry breath snorts in the
field gate. The May moon glosses black hide, then
the bare tarmac of a straight run for home.

Di Fronte

The cattle have been driven by routes
through open glades or by tracks through reeds
to arrive here, to make this their stand,
in front of the temple. Have they? Sure
of the temple? The carving movements
of insects might have crumbled the dust
that packs in the joints between slabs. Those
impeccable, fantasy insects.
No actual cattle. Our remarks take
shape near to each other, although
you have ducked into the store for our
provisions. Yet one would have thought that
there was no room for strong polychromes
in the white line-up, Istrian, which
best would serve as a principle of
orchestration, this October, this
late in the day, for describing more
than just the original primo,
while a shadow, cobalt-turquoise, draws
off the whole façade as if it were
translating it to a spirit world,
even as the last sun, cadmium,
touches the skin of the west side of
the dome and fetches it back closer.
From the fourteenth step, on the flyleaf
of my diary, with an old green
pencil, I map the squares, hexagons,
triangles, diamonds, the paving
of the small campo, until I have
figured it out, then rule off on the
edge of the canal. Emerald weed,
blackened, lifts and flaps, gulps and whacks on
the water-stairs, bobbed by the wake of
The Brilliance of the Seas, and the

properties snort and toss, envious
of the cuts that deny them and of
the goodness they have to rely on.
Attenzione! Nevertheless
ants do collect confetti, wrestling
grains of rice into cracks. A rounded
stanchion perks up to answer a small
oblong notice that shines on a door.
Messor barbara, I decide. Neat
repercussions. Present conjunctions.
Pizza capricciosa. An owl
imagines us. She is so far from
the truth! She is this immense blue-grey
facial disk with its eyes closed! And we
await her stare! She is the temple
façade with a triple pediment.
Is she not? She, at last, is the strong
phantasy, and to prosper she will
need to peck up the bits there could be
when the stars come out. Meanwhile it is
clear why the stanchion stiffens and the
notice presses itself against the
door. How swells sledge clean sheets off the treads,
and swill their slops on the risers. The
heifers have silken flanks. The owl dreams
that I descend a step and close my
diary. I snap it shut and it
becomes a rectangle to contain
the rest of the geometry, loose
chattels that could remain. Dolci with
tortiglione. And, stem to stern
hung with coloured lights, a cruise liner
from Nassau. It's all that I can have.

At South Elmham Minster

Talk to mother. Speak in a natural
easy voice, cruising the words. *Cirrus* and
thistles. Thiskin. Largesse. Debonair. Then
oaks and *hornbeams* and *forever.* Say that
oaks and hornbeams have been here forever,
in place, in motion, so what is it could
make us jealous? They strew largesse, each bit
of trash confirmed on its shadow. The clouds
likewise. The trees move on them. Cirrus roves
and curls. Tell her so. Pieces of mother.
We pinch the heads of the meadow thistles
so we can sniff honey on our fingers,
discovering mother, come in tatters,
pounced by thistles, brushed by shadows, all in
rapport, mother in her own ways. Thiskin.
We move on south, through the Snappage, into
Minster. We have nothing in the down. We
down nothing in the have. No debt and no
custody. Heyday and hurry ahead
every step of the way. In Sand Pit Close
two hares are chased by a black dog. They go
stiff-legged, ears up, only cruising, mild and
easy. Later, forth with all, they fool their
time away, flare, flaunt themselves, forget the
dog and punch the air, or ho, upstarted,
erect, distinct, and checked as the twelve stars
in the winter night, under the feet of
Orion. Clever in an empty space.
Come on, Keep moving. Hold the voice and line
length steady. Say that mother is out there,
and she is thiswise, thissen, thiskin, which
is thistles, cirrus cruising *de bonne aire.*

To a Nightingale

Nothing along the road. But
petals, maybe. Pink behind
and white inside. Nothing but
the coping of a bridge. Mutes
on the bricks, hard as putty,
then, in the sun, as metal.
Burls of *Grimmia,* hairy,
hoary, with their seed-capsules
uncurling. Red mites bowling
about on the baked lichen
and what look like casual
landings, striped flies, *Helina,*
Phaonia, could they be?
This month the lemon, I'll say
primrose-coloured, moths, which flinch
along the hedge then turn in
to hide, are Yellow Shells not
Shaded Broad-bars. Lines waver.
Camptogramma. Heat off the
road and the nick-nack of names.
Scotopteryx. Darkwing. The
flutter. Doubles and blurs the
margin. Fuscous and white. Stop
at nothing. To stop here at
nothing, as a chaffinch sings
interminably, all day.
A chiff-chaff. Purring of two
turtle doves. Voices, and some
vibrate with tenderness. I
say none of this for love. It
is anyone's giff-gaff. It
is anyone's quelque chose.
No business of mine. Mites which
ramble. Caterpillars which
curl up as question marks. Then
one note, five times, louder each
time, followed, after a fraught

pause, by a soft cuckle of
wet pebbles, which I could call
a glottal rattle. I am
empty, stopped at nothing, as
I wait for this song to shoot.
The road is rising as it
passes the apple tree and
makes its approach to the bridge.

Notes

'To explain anything we go back'
– Adrian Stokes[1]

R.F. Langley kept a record of the reading and journal entries that informed his published poems in three handwritten notebooks. Although he did not include any notes in his various collections, he often selected passages from these books at readings by way of prefacing a poem. He also alluded to much of the material contained in the first notebook during the interview he gave to *Angel Exhaust* magazine in 1996, when asked for a 'thread outside the labyrinth' of each of his *Twelve Poems* (1994). Langley obliged, but expressed a hope that 'the reader could miss almost everything and still get something out of it', adding: 'I don't like to give away too much. I don't like to surrender'.[2] With the ambivalence of these remarks in mind, these notes have been compiled as a bibliography of source texts for individual poems. As such, they are intended as signposts to further reading rather than explanatory apparatus. Readers who follow them will often recognise passages echoed or even quoted verbatim in the poem. But the wider context of the journal entry, essay, chapter, or book is also – as Langley observes at one point – 'most suggestive'.

The mass of material in the first notebook appears to date from a period of sustained reconstruction in the 1990s of the sources of *Twelve Poems* and the poems added to them by *Jack* (1998). The two later notebooks cover the poems collected in *The Face of It* (2007) and most of the uncollected verse to 2010. Over this period, Langley became increasingly punctilious about recording sources at the moment of composition, although material still occasionally turns up out of sequence, suggesting that he was looking back from a later date or forward to a future poem. In 2007, he described his practice as follows:

> When I finish a poem I always sit back and make notes on the sources, however simplistic, of the piece, keeping a copy of what seems useful in a notebook, in several notebooks now, because I find that I often forget where notions and phrases come from. These provide rich pickings for me later on, and useful remarks if

I have to give a reading, for instance. I might even feel that they are as interesting as the poem itself. They have authority, reach beyond what I did with them. I don't note what comes from Shakespeare, but most other sources get recorded.[3]

Shakespeare was not included because, as Langley said in 1996, the encounter with 'the same small number of plays' in his working life as a teacher 'fed me, as it were, day by day', providing a bedrock that 'cuts through and underlies the whole lot'.[4] To a later interviewer, he observed:

> I taught Shakespeare for forty years and think about him all the time. Almost every piece I write contains his ideas, my application of what I take to be his ideas, quotations from him and so on.[5]

Etymological dictionaries were also an important prompt, and the notebooks cite the chief of these: the fourth edition of W.W. Skeat's *An Etymological Dictionary of the English Language* (1910). The evolution of a word was, Langley said, something he allowed to 'lead' the writing process: 'The words I use are etymologically relevant. Always. [...] In addition to the virtue of direct experience, I want to feel to some extent, authorized by etymology.'[6] He brought the same attentiveness to bear on the close reading of poetry, as his friend Jeremy Prynne recalls: '[Roger] understood how words would individually find their place, to communicate their active bearing upon each other, often lighting on points of idiom to discover small windows opening out into complex vistas, "grass-roots" working'.

The notebooks do not contain the complete account of any poem's inspiration – the sprite-like figure of 'Man Jack', for example, was partly prompted by 'the dozens of columns in the *Oxford* [English] *Dictionary* on the word "Jack"'.[7] But they do set out Langley's main sources of material for composition: the autobiographical and the bibliographical – or, as he put it in a note, 'the interplay of ecstasies and inventories'. The opening quotation of the first notebook seems in particular to comment on the way in which 'direct experience' is enhanced by literary activity in the largest sense. It is the conclusion of Michael J. Roberts' preface to *The Spiders of Great Britain and Ireland* (1985):

> As a young naturalist, I always thought it a great pleasure, almost adventure, to find a plant or animal in the field and then go

home and find an illustration or description of it in a book. There is a real sense of someone having 'been there before' and, in an otherwise rapidly changing world, these small things can sometimes give a sense of stability.[8]

Towards the end of the third notebook, Langley appended an unusually extended comment to one of his own poems of natural observation, 'Videlicet', relating the poetic process to something like Roberts' 'sense of stability'. After quoting psychoanalyst Marion Milner's characterisation of alchemy as the quest for a state of mind in which 'the whole world seemed new created',[9] he adds:

> And now one might chance that the new creation, thus psychologically conceived, is the world as a place to dwell as indicated by Heidegger. That the organic images arrive often surprisingly, when one has expected some other outcome but has given careful attention so that they sort themselves out otherwise... [...] The words need suffusing with the event of the image.

'The event of the image' is something that Langley frequently discovered in the detailed scrutiny of a scene or object, as recorded in his journals. His borrowings from other authors often take the form of phrasing that gives life to a particular feeling or idea. The opening line of 'The Upshot', for example – 'We leave unachieved in the summer dusk' – is a quotation from Proust that caught the poet's ear 'because it's so unassertive and yet it's got such fine syllabic things going quietly in it and it's also so sad'.[10] The specific English cadence of the quotation is taken from Elliott Coleman's translation of *Studies in Human Time* by Georges Poulet, who comments on the whole passage: 'Moments unachieved in their time, slender and linear [...] seemed, however, to give the present a consistence, a reality that they themselves did not possess'.[11] These notes direct readers towards such contexts where they are known (editions and translations have been identified where possible). For the small number of poems that have not been indexed to any passage, no further comment is offered.

The journal entries, cited here simply by date, have all been copied into the notebooks from the extensive autobiographical prose that Langley regarded as a way of bringing 'the outside world in'.[12] Introducing a selected volume of *Journals* in 2006, he noted that although 'sometimes the poems feed directly off the journals [...] they have to do with experience in their own way, which is obviously not that of the journals'.[13] They should not, therefore, be regarded as 'first draft' poems, although readers will undoubtedly discover correspondences between the poems and the entries that appeared in *Journals* and in *PN Review* magazine. These, however, were often excerpted and revised from longer reflections for the same date. Other entries remain unpublished.

Only one journal entry in the notebooks comments explicitly on a poem in progress ('Depending on the Weather'). Dated 17 June 2002, it offers a suggestive illustration of how the poems respond to 'experience in their own way':

> I have 19 lines of a poem unexpectedly triggered after months... of nothing... triggered by the tiger beetle running at the sand wasp as we walked round the woods to Dunwich Heath the other day. Why did that work at all? Not the ant-lions, seen on the same walk. The beetle. Something of its movement before I knew what it was – while it was too far off to even see it was green. Its speed and probing run. Its consciousness, seen in its lifted head.

In the opening lines of the poem, this is transformed into an image of the reading mind:

> The hurry to bite that runs over the spare
> text, with his head high, with his bulging eyes.

The running-ahead of questing consciousness is also what caught Langley's eye in works of fiction, philosophy, literary criticism, biography, art history, popular science, and psychology (although Langley's poems are often in conversation with the poets he admired, he rarely cites verse in these notebooks). His own list of 'a few books I read often' ran as follows:

> Any Klein and Winnicott. Wittgenstein in bits. Iris Murdoch: *The Sovereignty of Good*, and *Existentialists and Mystics*. W.R. Bion: *Attention and Interpretation*. Thomas Nagel: *Mortal Questions*, *The View from Nowhere*. Keir Elam: *Shakespeare's Universe of Discourse*. John Cage: *Silence, A Year from Monday*. Richard Wollheim: *The Thread of Life, Painting as an Art, The Mind and its Depths, On the Emotions*. Richard Cody: *The Landscape of the Mind*. Merleau-Ponty: *The Phenomenology of Perception*. Adam

Phillips: *Promises, Promises.* Any work by Adrian Stokes, especially *The Quattrocento, Colour and Form*, and the later psychological essays, *The Image in Form* etc. Marion Milner: *A Life of One's Own.* Elizabeth Sewell: *The Field of Nonsense.* Robert Bresson: *Notes on the Cinematographer.* Keith Thomas: *Religion and the Decline of Magic*, etc etc.[14]

The pre-eminent writer and thinker for Langley here is Adrian Stokes (1902–1972), whose art criticism was, he said, 'the first coherent aesthetic that I'd ever met'.[15] His deep and repeated reading of Stokes runs through the oeuvre, prompting journal entries and poems. In a letter from 2005 about his poem 'The Bellini in San Giovanni Crisostomo' – which meditates on a painting in Venice that he 'spent a day with' – Langley observed that 'it implies, if one wants it to, a number of the best insights of Stokes and Wollheim, *applied*, as it were, rather than explained'.[16]

The notebooks feature a number of quotations from Stokes that are not cited as source material for poems, but which implicitly illuminate aspects of Langley's own aesthetic. To read Stokes' prose is to gain a more profound insight into the thinking behind these poems than any conventional annotation could offer. At the start of the first notebook, for example, Langley quotes the final sentence of the following paragraph from Stokes' essay 'Form in Art':

> Form bestows not only pattern but completeness, not only the sense of separate life, but the sense of fusion. In art, repose will in some manner encompass energy. This point is crucial. Whatever the rhythm, the force, the fierceness, the furore, there is yet calm, for there is also completeness. An identity has been established amid the manifold to whose differences full value is given: just as a mirror's surface makes more comprehensive the turbulent scene reflected there.[17]

On the first page of the first notebook, Stokes' recollections of 'Living in Ticino, 1947–50' provide an epigraph to the complete undetaking: 'To explain anything we go back' (see above). On the same page there is a single untitled paragraph in Langley's hand. This appears to be an unpublished – even private – prose poem, placed at the head of the notebook as a self-portrait of the poet. Written with the rhythmic phrasing, play of rhyme, and compression of reference that characterises Langley's verse, it invokes the medieval

French legend of the fight between the knight Oliver and the giant Fierabras, using a form of words that points to at least one identifiable source. In the Reverend Alfred J. Church's *Stories from Charlemagne* (1902), a book for children, Oliver says to Fierebras: 'I will make no agreement with you, save this: that I will do my best to slay you, and you shall do the same with me'. As a child, Langley and his brothers played games with their own intricately-carved medieval knights, and the dream-world of childhood mythology is never far away in these poems. Here, the recalled phrase is repurposed – as so often in Langley's literary bricolage – to reflect on the relationship between reader and writer in the alchemical work of remembering and imagining:

> I thought of myself as thinking I knew myself, again, by the way it was done, and cleared and called out, christened and cleared out. I thought of myself as having done that much. Here at the outer edge, where the skirts fluttered, saying what I'd said. My list of names. Yes. When I'm working twenty years are as none. Oliver riding. Fierabras waiting at ease under the tree. Deeper darkness touches out the closer, paler rims. The curled toes, the tassels on the boots. Points of light to punctuate the pointless fight. I will make no agreement with you and you shall do the same with me. Agreed. Out of none was the way it was done. Causing me to do things, demanding that they should be done. Send me a white cane. I touch the grass here, here and here. And here. At the extra one, all four ignite. The one you turned back to give after the farewells were over.

Notes

1 Adrian Stokes, 'Living in Ticino, 1947–50', in *The Image in Form*, ed. Richard Wollheim (Harmondsworth: Penguin, 1972), pp. 314–20 (p. 316).
2 'R.F. Langley Interviewed by R.F. Walker', in *Don't Start Me Talking* (Cambridge: Salt, 2006), ed. Tim Allen and Andrew Duncan, pp. 237–57 (p. 243).
3 Personal correspondence, 3 November 2007.
4 'R.F. Langley Interviewed', p. 240.
5 Matías Serra Bradford, 'The Long Question of Poetry: A Quiz for R.F. Langley', *PN Review*, 199 (May–June 2011), pp.15–17 (p. 16).
6 'R.F. Langley Interviewed', p. 244.
7 'R.F. Langley Interviewed', p. 248.
8 Michael J. Roberts, *The Spiders of Great Britain and Ireland*, 3 vols (Colchester: Harley Books, 1985), III, p. 8.

9   Marion Milner ('Joanna Field'), *An Experiment in Leisure* (London: Chatto & Windus, 1937), pp. 153–55.
10 'R.F. Langley Interviewed', p. 244.
11 Georges Poulet, *Studies in Human Time*, trans. Elliott Coleman (Baltimore: Johns Hopkins University Press, 1956), p. 306.
12 'R.F. Langley Interviewed', p. 244.
13 R.F. Langley, *Journals* (Exeter: Shearsman, 2006), p. 7.
14 'The Long Question of Poetry', p. 16.
15 'R.F. Langley Interviewed', p. 241.
16 Personal correspondence, 28 December 2005.
17 Adrian Stokes, 'Form in Art', in *New Directions in Psycho-Analysis*, ed. Melanie Klein and others (London: Tavistock, 1955), pp. 406–20 (pp. 408–9).

❧

Note (1994): first published in *A Calendar of Modern Poetry*, ed. Michael Schmidt (1994).

Langley's 'Note' appeared alongside 'Mariana' and 'Juan Fernandez' in a special anthology edition of *PN Review*, published to mark the 100th issue of the magazine. A passage quoted from Michael Baxandall's *Patterns of Intention* (1985) in the first of Langley's notebooks attributes the remarks 'Every brush stroke changes the picture' to Cézanne and 'Don't talk to the driver!' to Picasso (see 'Mariana'). A further quotation from Baxandall is titled by Langley 'a sustained perceptual effort. Picasso', and followed by a set of bracketed comments, which include the observation 'all sequence poems – the interplay of ecstasies and inventories'. Below this are the journal entries by Ford Madox Brown for 1 September 1854 and 21 August 1855. Later in the notebook Langley quotes from W.W. Skeat's *An Etymological Dictionary of the English Language* (1910) on the etymology of 'toe', 'token', and 'teach' (see 'Juan Fernandez').

Epigraph

'The act of finding / What will suffice': Wallace Stevens, 'Of Modern Poetry' (1942). These words are written at the front of the folder in which Langley kept copies of all his published poems. They also appear as an epigraph to the third and final notebook. The drawing of an Athenian coin is by the author.

Man Jack: first published in *Poetical Histories*, 30 (Cambridge: P. Riley, 1993).

Journal, March 1991, August 1992.
Bion, W.R., *Attention and Interpretation* (1970), Chapter 11, 'Lies and the Thinker'.
Heidegger, Martin, 'The Thing', in *Poetry, Language, Thought*, trans. Albert Hofstadter (1971).
Locke, John, *On Human Understanding* (1689), Book One, Chapter 2, 'No Innate Principles in the Mind'.
Merleau-Ponty, Maurice, *Phenomenology of Perception*, trans. Colin Smith (1962), Part Two, Chapter 3, 'The Thing and the Natural World'.
Milner, Marion ('Joanna Field'), *A Life of One's Own* (1934; rev. edn 1952),

Chapter 4, 'The Coming and Going of Delight'.
Murdoch, Iris, *The Fire and the Sun* (1977).

Mariana: first published in *Arts Report*, May 1985.

Journal, 9 April 'onwards' 1983.
Baxandall, Michael, *Patterns of Intention* (1985), Chapter 2, 'Intentional Visual Interest: Picasso's *Portrait of Kahnweiler*'.
Bion, W.R., *Attention and Interpretation* (1970), Chapter 11, 'Lies and the Thinker'.
Cody, Richard, *The Landscape of the Mind* (1969), 'Conclusion'.
Jacobs, René, 'Introduction', *Monteverdi: Un Concert Spirituel*. Cond. René Jacobs. CD HMA 1901032. 1980.
Sartre, Jean-Paul, *The Psychology of Imagination* (1948), trans. Bernard Frechtman, Chapter 1, 'The Certain'.

The Upshot: first published in *Equofinality*, Spring/Summer 1984.

[The first notebook features two photographs of the 'Bohun' (south) aisle, St Andrew's church, Westhall, Suffolk, which have been captioned 'The Upshot'.]
Journal, 1976, April 1977, August 1981.
Bion, W.R., *Attention and Interpretation* (1970), Chapter 11, 'Lies and the Thinker'.
Gombrich, Ernst, 'Mirror and Map: Theories of Pictorial Representation', *Philosophical Transactions of the Royal Society of London, Biological Sciences*, 270 (1975).
Milner, Marion ('Joanna Field'), *A Life of One's Own* (1934; rev. edn 1952), Chapter 7, 'Two Ways of Looking'.
Miner, Earl Roy, *An Introduction to Japanese Court Poetry* (1968), Chapter 6, 'Major Poets from 1100 to 1241'.
Murdoch, Iris, *The Fire and the Sun* (1977).
Proust, Marcel, *À la recherche du temps perdu*, Volume One (*Du côté de chez Swann*), quoted in Georges Poulet, 'Proust', *Studies in Human Time*, trans. Elliott Coleman (1956).
Sartre, Jean-Paul, *La Nausée* (1938), '6 heures du soir' [the text is quoted in English but the translation has not been identified].
Stokes, Adrian, *Colour and Form* (1937), Chapter 3.
Stokes, Adrian, *Inside Out* (1947), Part One.
Stokes, Adrian, *The Quattro Cento* (1932), Part Two, Chapter 5, 'In Conclusion'.
Unger, Roberto Mangabeira, *Passion: An Essay on Personality* (1984), Chapter 1.

The Ecstasy Inventories: first published in *Hem* (1978).

Journal, August–September 1974, August 1975, and April 1977.
Dodds, E. R., *The Greeks and the Irrational* (1951), Chapter 5, 'The Greek Shamans and the Origin of Puritanism'.
Eliot, George, *Adam Bede* (1859), Chapter 1, quoted in Frank Kermode, *How We Read Novels* (The 4th Gwilym James Memorial Lecture, Southampton University, 1975).
Freud, Sigmund, 'Beyond the Pleasure Principle' (1920), in *The Standard Edition of the Complete Psychological Works of Sigmund Freud*, ed. James Strachey, 24 vols (1955), XVIII.
Grigson, Geoffrey, *The Englishman's Flora* (1958), entry for 'Elder'.

Hesse, Mary, 'In Defence of Objectivity', *Proceedings of the British Academy*, 58 (1972).

Plato, *Phaedrus*, in *Five Dialogues* (1952), trans. J. Wright, 229–30.

'The Roots of Writing', *Time*, 1 August 1977.

Sartre, Jean-Paul, *La Nausée* (1938), '6 heures du soir' [the text is quoted in English but the translation has not been identified].

Steer, Francis W., 'The Inventory of Arthur Coke of Bramfield, 1629', in *Proceedings of the Suffolk Institute of Archaeology*, 25 (1951). [The front and back cover of the first notebook feature photographic details of Nicholas Stone's memorial to Arthur and Elizabeth Coke in St Andrew's church, Bramfield, Suffolk.]

'Wolf warfare protects deer', *Science*, 21 October 1977.

Juan Fernandez: first published in *A Vision Very Like Reality*, December 1979.

Journal, 23 August–7 September 1974, 1976, April 1977, August–September 1978.

The Earl of Cranbrook, 'Suffolk Perambulations', *The Countryman*, Spring 1966.

Defoe, Daniel, *Robinson Crusoe* (1719), Chapter 11.

Heidegger, Martin, 'The Thing', in *Poetry, Language, Thought*, trans. Albert Hofstadter (1971).

Hesse, Mary, 'In Defence of Objectivity', *Proceedings of the British Academy*, 58 (1972).

Jung, Carl, *The Archetypes and the Collective Unconscious*, trans. R.F.C. Hull (1959), 'Archetypes of the Collective Unconscious'.

Kierkegaard, Søren, *Concluding Unscientific Postscript to the Philosophical Fragments*, trans. David F. Swenson and W. Lowrie (1941), Part Two, 2.3, 'Real or ethical subjectivity – the speculative thinker'.

Langer, Susanne K., *Feeling and Form* (1953), Chapter 6.

Lyotard, Jean-Francois, 'Newman: The Instant', in *The Inhuman* (1991), trans. Geoffrey Bennington and Rachel Bowlby.

Murdoch, Iris, *The Fire and the Sun* (1977).

Murdoch, Iris, 'The Sovereignty of Good over Other Concepts', in *The Sovereignty of Good* (1970).

Plato, *Phaedrus*, in *Five Dialogues* (1952), trans. J. Wright, 250.

'The Roots of Writing', *Time*, 1 August 1977.

Skeat, W.W., *An Etymological Dictionary of the English Language*, 4th edn (1910), entries for 'toe', 'token', 'teach'.

Matthew Glover: first published in *Hem* (1978).

Clare, John, journal entry, 29 September 1824, quoted in W.G. Hoskins, *The Making of the English Landscape* (1955), Chapter 6, 'Parliamentary Enclosure and the Landscape'.

Eliade, Mircea, *The Sacred and the Profane*, trans. Willard R. Trask (1959), Chapter 1, 'Sacred Space and Making the World Sacred'.

Gould, James T., *Men of Aldridge* (1957), Chapter 7, 'The Farmers'.

Saxon Landings: first published in *Hem* (1978).

[The inside back cover of the second notebook features a postcard showing the face of Oceanus from the Great Dish in the Mildenhall treasure at the British

Museum (Roman Britain, 4th century AD)]

The British Museum, *The Mildenhall Treasure: A Handbook* (1964)

Holman Hunt, William, *Pre-Raphaelitism and the Pre-Raphaelite Brotherhood* (1905), Chapter 13, '1853–1854'.

Stokes, Adrian, *Inside Out* (1947), Part One.

Arbor Low: first published as a Cambridge Poetry Festival poster poem, 1983.

Journal, 18 May 1969.

The Long History of Heresy: first published in *Holophrase*, c. 1980.

Journal, August–September 1979

Bion, W.R., *Attention and Interpretation* (1970).

Brown, Ford Madox, journal entries for 1 September 1854–21 August 1855, in *Pre-Raphaelite Diaries and Letters*, ed. W.M. Rosetti (1900).

Coleridge, Samuel Taylor, 'The Nightingale. Written in April, 1798'.

Freud, Sigmund, 'Beyond the Pleasure Principle' (1920), in *The Standard Edition of the Complete Psychological Works of Sigmund Freud*, ed. James Strachey, 24 vols (1955), XVIII.

Hardy, Thomas, *Far from the Madding Crowd* (1874), Chapter 22.

Kagemusha. Dir. Akira Kurosawa. Toho Company and Twentieth Century Fox Film Corporation, 1980. [A still depicting the hero of this film, taken from a newspaper, is pasted onto a page of the first notebook. The phrase 'under the roar walls' and the title of this poem have been written next to it. Langley described the image in interview as 'the prince-figure [...] on horseback followed by his retinue going past an enormous stone wall' ('R.F. Langley Interviewed', p. 253)].

Lévi-Strauss, Claude, *Totemism*, trans. Rodney Needham (1963), Chapter 5, 'Totemism from Within'.

Munro, Lois, 'Steps in Ego-Integration Observed in Play-Analysis', in *New Directions in Psycho-Analysis*, ed. Melanie Klein and others (1955).

Murdoch, Iris, *The Fire and the Sun* (1977).

Suzuki, D.T., *Zen and Japanese Culture* (1938; 2nd edn, 1959), Chapter 6, 'Zen and Swordsmanship / II'.

Blithing: first published in *Hem* (1978).

Evans, George Ewart, *Ask the Fellows Who Cut the Hay* (1956), Chapter 24, 'Villlage Legends, Customs and Superstitions'.

Frazer, J.G., *The Golden Bough*, 2 vols (1890), II, Chapter 10.3, 'Eating the God'.

Rough Silk: first published in *Sidelong* (1981).

Journal, August 1976.

Cézanne, Paul, conversation with Joachim Gasquet, quoted in Adrian Stokes, *Cézanne* (1947), 'Introduction'.

The Gorgoneion: first published in *Equofinality*, Spring/Summer 1984.

Journal, 18 August–1 September 1974, August 1979, August 1982.

Cézanne, Paul, conversation with Joachim Gasquet, quoted in Adrian Stokes, *Cézanne* (1947), 'Introduction'.

Eliot, George, *Middlemarch* (1871–72), Chapter 83.

Miner, Earl Roy, *An Introduction to Japanese Court Poetry* (1968), Chapter 6, 'Major Poets from 1100 to 1241'.

Murdoch, Iris, *The Fire and the Sun* (1977).

Jack's Pigeon: first published in *PN Review*, January–February 1996.

Journal, August 1980, August 1988, August 1991.

Bashō, Matsuo, 'The Records of a Weather-Exposed Skeleton', in *The Narrow Road to the Deep North and Other Travel Sketches*, trans. Nobuyuki Yuasa (1966).

Milner, Marion ('Joanna Field'), *An Experiment in Leisure* (1937), Chapters 15 and 16.

Milner, Marion ('Joanna Field'), *A Life of One's Own* (1934; rev. edn 1952), Chapter 4, 'The Coming and Going of Delight'.

Stokes, Adrian, 'Living in Ticino, 1947–50', *Art and Literature*, 1 (1964).

Poor Moth: first published in *PN Review*, March–April 1998.

Journal, 4 August 1990.

Camus, Albert, *The Myth of Sisyphus* (1955), trans. Justin O'Brien, 'Absurd Creation: Kirilov'.

Ferguson, Frances, *Wordsworth: Language as Counter-Spirit* (1977), Chapter 1, 'Writing About Language: Wordsworth's Prose'.

Hume, David, *A Treatise of Human Nature* (1738), Book 1, 4.7, quoted in Thomas Nagel, 'The Absurd', *Mortal Questions* (1979).

Milner, Marion ('Joanna Field'), *A Life of One's Own* (1934; rev. edn 1952), Chapter 4, 'The Coming and Going of Delight'.

Nagel, Thomas, 'Subjective and Objective', 'The Absurd', and 'What is it like to be a bat?', in *Mortal Questions* (1979).

Stokes, Adrian, 'On Being Taken Out of Oneself', in *A Game That Must Be Lost: Collected Papers* (1973), ed. Eric Rhode.

Wittgenstein, Ludwig, *Philosophical Investigations*, 2nd edn, trans. G.E.M. Anscombe (1958), Part One, 610.

The Night Piece: first published in *The Gig*, March 1999.

Hertz, Neil, 'Wordsworth and the Tears of Adam', in *The End of the Line: Essays on Psychoanalysis and the Sublime* (1985).

The Barber's Beard: first published in Peter Riley, *A Poetry in Favour of the World* (Form Books Occasional Paper, 6, 1997).

Journal, 17 February 1996.

Encyclopaedia Britannica, 15th edn (1974), entry for 'Scipio'.

'Hyakujo's Fox', in *Zen Flesh, Zen Bones*, ed. and trans. Paul Reps and Nyogen Senzaki (1957).

Lyotard, Jean-Francois, 'Newman: The Instant', in *The Inhuman*, trans. Geoffrey Bennington and Rachel Bowlby (1991).

Milner, Marion ('Joanna Field'), *A Life of One's Own* (1934; rev. edn 1952),

Chapter 4, 'The Coming and Going of Delight'.

Parkinson, John, *Paradisi in Sole Paradisus Terrestris* (1629), entry for 'Allisanders'.

Stokes, Adrian, *Reflections on the Nude* (1967), in *The Critical Writings of Adrian Stokes*, ed. Lawrence Gowing, 3 vols (1978), III, 'The Image in Form'.

Wollheim, Richard, *The Thread of Life* (1986), Chapter 3, 'Iconicity, Imagination, and Desire'.

Tom Thumb: first published in Peter Riley, *A Poetry in Favour of the World* (Form Books Occasional Paper, 6, 1997).

Journal, August 1995.

Apel, Willi, *Harvard Dictionary of Music*, 2nd edn (1970), entry for 'bowing'.

Bashō, Matsuo, 'The Records of a Weather-Exposed Skeleton', in *The Narrow Road to the Deep North and Other Travel Sketches*, trans. Nobuyuki Yuasa (1966).

Langer, Suzanne K., *Philosophy in a New Key*, 2nd edn (1951), Chapter 8, 'On Significance in Music'.

Milner, Marion ('Joanna Field'), *A Life of One's Own* (1934; rev. edn 1952), Chapter 4, 'The Coming and Going of Delight'.

Nagel, Thomas, 'Fodor: The Boundaries of Inner Space' and 'Searle: Why We Are Not Computers', in *Other Minds* (1995).

Wittgenstein, Ludwig, *Philosophical Investigations*, 2nd edn, trans. G.E.M. Anscombe (1958), Part One, 601–05.

Cakes and Ale: first published in *PN Review*, July–August 2000.

Cook Ting: first published as 'Rauschenberg' in *April Eye: Poems for Peter Riley* (*infernal methods*, 2000).

Cage, John, 'On Robert Rauschenberg, Artist, and His Work', in *Silence* (1968).

Chuang Tzu, *Basic Writings*, trans. Burton Watson (1964), Section 3, 'The Secret of Caring for Life'.

Cocker, Mark, 'Trouble in the air as pirates go raiding in Sizewell's shadow', *Guardian*, 4 Feb 2000.

Rauschenberg, Robert, 'Fulton Street studio view, artist's domestic alcove, c. 1953' including 'Untitled [paper sculpture], c. 1953 / Hanging assemblage: balsa wood, paper, and twine / c. 20 x 40 x 15 in. / Lost or destroyed', in Hopps, W., *Robert Rauschenberg: The Early 1950s* (1991).

Rauschenberg, Robert, 'Untitled (*Scatole Personali* series), c. 1952 / Assemblage: lidded painted wood box with twig and beetle / 1½ x 3 x 2⅛ in. (closed) / Collection of the artist, New York', in Hopps, W., *Robert Rauschenberg: The Early 1950s* (1991).

Experiment with a Hand Lens: first published in *Oxford Poetry*, Summer 2001.

Journal, 14 February 1998.

Sixpence a Day: first published in *PN Review* 139, May–June 2001.

Journal, 14 May 2000.

Fabre, Augustin, *The Life of Jean Henri Fabre, the Entomologist, 1823–1910*, trans.

Bernard Miall (1921), Chapter 17.

Still Life With Wineglass: first published in *London Review of Books*, 21 June 2001.

Journal, 6–8 March 2001.

Cézanne, Paul, conversation with Joachim Gasquet, quoted in Adrian Stokes, *Cézanne* (1947), 'Introduction'.

Phillips, Adam, 'Narcissism, For and Against', in *Promises, Promises* (2000).

Rosenberg, Harold, 'Icon Maker: Barnett Newman', in *The De-definition of Art: Action Art to Pop to Earthworks* (1972).

Stokes, Adrian, *Inside Out* (1947), Part One.

Sylvester, David, *Looking at Giacometti* (1994), Chapter 5, 'The Residue of Vision'.

Winnicott, D.W., *Playing and Reality* (1971), quoted in Adam Phillips, 'Poetry and Psychoanalysis', *Promises, Promises* (2000).

No Great Shakes: first published in *PN Review*, July–August 2000.

Simons, Paul, 'On the trail of the lonesome pine cone', *Guardian*, 24 January 1986.

After the Funeral: first published in *PN Review*, September–October 2002.

Journal, 9 November 1997.

Hoffmann, Michael, 'Slowly / Swiftly' [review of James Schuyler, *Last Poems* and *Alfred and Guinevere*], *London Review of Books*, 7 February 2002.

Scott, Rosemary E., *Percival David Foundation of Chinese Art: A Guide to the Collection* (1989), 'The Wares of North China in the Northern Song and the Jin Dynasty'.

Sewell, Elizabeth, *The Field of Nonsense* (1952), Chapter 14, 'Will You, Won't You?'.

Depending on the Weather: first published in *Stand*, 4.4/5.1 (2003).

Journal, 17 June 2002.

Thomas, Keith, *Religion and the Decline of Magic* (1991), Chapters 14–18, 'Witchcraft'.

Wollheim, Richard, *The Thread of Life* (1984), Chapter 3, 'Iconicity, Imagination, and Desire'.

Blues for Titania: first published in *London Review of Books*, 24 July 2003.

Bastin, Harold, 'War and Peace in Nature', in *The Wonders of Nature*, illus. C.F. Tunnicliffe (1940).

Berger, John, 'Brancusi', in *The Shape of a Pocket* (2001).

Juvenal, *Satires*, 15, quoted in Barbara Watterson, *Gods of Ancient Egypt* (1984), 'Introduction'.

Plesters, Joyce, 'Investigation of Materials and Techniques', in David Bull and Joyce Plesters, *The Feast of the Gods: Conservation, Examination, and Interpretation* (1990).

Stokes, Adrian, 'Notes' to *Michelangelo* (1955), in *The Critical Writings of Adrian Stokes*, ed. Lawrence Gowing, 3 vols (1978), III, Note 1.

My Moth: My Song: first published in *PN Review*, January–February 2004.

Emmet, A. Maitland, *The Scientific Names of the British Lepidoptera: Their History and Meaning* (1991).

Fowles, John, *The Tree* (1979), quoted in *The Oxford Book of Nature Writing*, ed. Richard Mabey (1995).

Homer, *The Iliad*, trans. E.V. Rieu (1950), Books 10 and 11.

Murdoch, Iris, 'Nostalgia for the Particular' (1952), in *Existentialists and Mystics: Writings on Philosophy and Literature*, ed. Peter J. Conradi (1997).

Wollheim, Richard, *Painting as an Art* (1987), 'Preface'.

Cash Point: first published in *London Review of Books*, 3 June 2004.

Elam, Keir, *Shakespeare's Universe of Discourse* (1984), Chapter 3, 'Signs'.

Skeat, W.W., *An Etymological Dictionary of the English Language*, 4th edn (1910), entry for 'mystery'.

Touchstone: first published in *PN Review*, January–February 2005.

Journal, 23 August 2003.

James, William, *The Varieties of Religious Experience* (1902), Lecture 20, 'Conclusions'.

Rundle, Bede, *Why There Is Something Rather Than Nothing* (2004), Chapter 5, 'Essence and Existence' and Chapter 7, 'Mind and Agency'.

Brute Conflict: first published in *PN Review*, November–December 2005.

Klein, Melanie, 'The Psycho-Analytic Play Technique', in *The Selected Melanie Klein*, ed. Juliet Mitchell (1986).

Lockwood, W.B., *The Oxford Book of British Bird Names* (1984), entries for 'Starling' and 'Stare'.

Miner, Earl Roy, *An Introduction to Japanese Court Poetry* (1968), Chapter 6, 'Major Poets from 1100 to 1241'.

Peacock, Irvine, *The Secret Life of Objects* (2004).

Skeat, W.W., *An Etymological Dictionary of the English Language*, 4th edn (1910), entries for 'believe', 'lief', 'desire', 'calculate'.

Stokes, Adrian, 'On Being Taken Out of Oneself', in *A Game That Must Be Lost: Collected Papers*, ed. Eric Rhode (1973).

Wollheim, Richard, *The Thread of Life* (1984), Chapter 2, 'On the Mind' and Chapter 6, 'The Examined Life'.

Skrymir's Glove: first published in *London Review of Books*, 16 December 2004.

[The inside cover of the third notebook features a postcard of The Angel Hotel in Halesworth, Suffolk, which has been captioned 'Skrymir's Glove'.]

Bryson, Norman, *Vision and Painting* (1983), Chapter 2, 'The Essential Copy'.

Davies, Malcolm, 'Stesichorus' *Geryoneis* and its Folk-Tale Origins', *The Classical Quarterly*, 38 (1988).

Husserl, Edmund, quoted in Norman Bryson, *Vision and Painting* (1983), Chapter 1, 'The Natural Attitude'.

Perloff, Marjorie, 'The Word as Such: L=A=N=G=U=A=G=E Poetry in the

Eighties', in *The Dance of the Intellect* (1985).

Skeat, W.W., *An Etymological Dictionary of the English Language*, 4th edn (1910), entry for 'real'.

Wollheim, Richard, *Painting as an Art* (1987), Chapter 3, 'The Spectator in the Picture, Friedrich, Manet, Hals'.

At Sotterley: first published in *London Review of Books*, 21 July 2005.

Bresson, Robert, *Notes on the Cinematographer*, trans. Jonathan Griffin (1986).

Caravaggio: The Final Years, guide to the National Gallery exhibition, 23 February–22 May 2005.

Luke: 10. 40–42.

Wollheim, Richard, *Painting as an Art* (1987), Chapter 2, 'What the Spectator Sees'.

The Bellini in San Giovanni Crisostomo: first published in *London Review of Books*, 6 April 2006.

Stokes, Adrian, *The Invitation in Art* (1965), Chapter 3, 'Landscape, Art, and Ritual'.

Wollheim, Richard, *Painting as an Art* (1987), Chapter 6, 'Painting, Metaphor, and the Body: Titian, Bellini, De Kooning, etc'.

Wollheim, Richard, *The Thread of Life* (1984), Chapter 7, 'From Voices to Values: The Growth of the Moral Sense'

Birdwatching Poem: first published in *PN Review*, July–August 2006.

[The inside cover of the second notebook features a postcard of the mummy-portrait of a youth from the collection of the Sainsbury Centre for Visual Arts, University of East Anglia, Norwich (Egypt, c. AD 100, wax encaustic on wood panel, h. 40.6 cm). Such works are often known as 'Fayum' portraits, after their place of origin.]

Journal, 3 March 2006.

Il Redentore: first published in *The Face of It* (2007).

Journal, 24–25 March and 1 April 2006

Wittkower, Rudolf, *Architectural Principles in the Age of Humanism*, 4th edn (1988), Part 4, 'The Problem of Harmonic Proportion in Architecture'.

Stokes, Adrian, *Greek Culture and the Ego* (1958).

The Wall Tomb of Giacomo Surian: first published in *The Face of It* (2007).

Miller, Jonathan, 'An Analysis of Social Activity: Dialogue with Rom Harré', in *States of Mind* (1983).

Achilles: first published in *The Face of It* (2007).

Journal, 6 May 1996, 8 August 2005, 4 June 2006.

Gage, John, *Colour and Meaning: Art, Science and Symbolism* (1999), Chapter 4, 'Colour in History – Relative and Absolute' and Chapter 5, 'Colour-words and

Colour-patches'.

Hardy, Thomas, *Tess of the d'Urbervilles* (1891), Chapter 20.

Heidegger, Martin, 'The Origin of the Work of Art', in *Poetry, Language, Thought*, trans. Albert Hofstadter (1971).

Newton, Isaac, 'Hypothesis explaining the properties of light' (1675), in *Papers and Letters on Natural Philosophy*, 2nd edn, ed. I.B. Cohen (1978).

Oliver, Douglas, 'Three Lilies', in *Poets on Writing: Britain 1970-1991*, ed. Denise Riley (1992).

Pollitt, J.J., *Art and Experience in Classical Greece* (1972), Chapter 2, 'Consciousness and Conscience: The Early Classical Period, c. 480–450 B.C.'.

Verity, Enid, *Colour* (1967), Chapter 10, 'Colour and Light' and Chapter 14, 'The Psychological Perception of Colour'.

Spoken Soon: first published in *The Face of It* (2007). Originally titled 'Wild Strawberries' in notebook references.

Journal, 25 and 28 June 2006.

Bergman, Ingmar, *The Seventh Seal* (1957), in *Four Screenplays of Ingmar Bergman*, trans. David Kushner and Lars Malmström (1960).

Bergman, Ingmar, *Wild Strawberries* (1957), in *Four Screenplays* (1960).

Skeat, W.W., *An Etymological Dictionary of the English Language*, 4th edn (1910), entry for 'spick and span'.

Stokes, Adrian, *Three Essays on the Painting of Our Time* (1961), Chapter 2, 'Some Connections and Differences Between Visionary and Aesthetic Experience'.

You with Your Visions and Dreams: unpublished. Written in November 2010 for inclusion in a proposed book of portraits of contemporary poets by the photographer Jemimah Kuhfeld.

Aftermath: first published in *An Unofficial Roy Fisher*, ed. Peter Robinson (Exeter: Shearsman, 2010).

Fisher, Roy, '"They Are All Gone Into the World": Roy Fisher in Conversation with Peter Robinson', in *Interviews Through Time, and Selected Prose*, ed. Tony Frazer (2000).

The Best Piece of Sculpture in Perugia: first published in *London Review of Books*, 5 July 2007.

[The third notebook features a photograph captioned 'The Best Piece of Sculpture in Perugia'. It shows the marble relief known as 'The Obedience', by Agostino di Duccio, on the façade of the Oratorio San Bernardino, Perugia.]

Buckley, Jonathan, and others, *The Rough Guide to Tuscany and Umbria*, 6th edn (2006), entry for Perugia.

Leder, Drew, *The Absent Body* (1990), Chapter 6, 'To Form One Body'.

Stokes, Adrian, 'On Resignation', in *A Game That Must Be Lost: Collected Papers*, ed. Eric Rhode (1973).

In the Bowels of the Lower Cave: first published in *PN Review*, July–August 2008.

Eastham, Anne and Michael, 'The Wall Art of the Franco-Cantabrian Deep Caves', *Art History*, 2 (December 1979).

Laming, Annette, *Lascaux: Paintings and Engravings*, trans. Eleanore Frances Armstrong (1959), Chapter 5, 'The Purpose and Meaning of the Paintings and Engravings'.

Videlicet: first published in *London Review of Books*, 31 July 2008.

Barthes, Roland, 'So', in *Empire of Signs*, trans. Richard Howard (1983).

Grigson, Geoffrey, *The Englishman's Flora* (1958), entry for 'White Dead Nettle'.

Heidegger, Martin, 'The Origin of the Work of Art', in *Poetry, Language, Thought* (1971), trans. Albert Hofstadter.

Hutchinson, John, *British Wild Flowers*, 2 vols (1955), entries for 'Chickweed' and 'Red Dead Nettle'.

Milner, Marion ('Joanna Field'), *An Experiment in Leisure* (1937), Chapter 13.

Milner, Marion, *On Not Being Able to Paint* (1950), quoted in Adam Phillips, 'Clutter: A Case History', *Promises, Promises* (2000).

Suzuki, D.T., *Zen and Japanese Culture* (1938; 2nd edn, 1959), Chapter 7, 'Zen and Haiku'.

Ueda, Makoto, *Bashō and His Interpreters* (1992), 'Road to the North 1689–1691' and 'Two Western Journeys 1684–1688'.

Practical Myth-Making: first published in *London Review of Books*, 8 October 2009.

Bergson, Henri, *The Two Sources of Morality and Religion*, trans. R.A. Audra and Cloudesley Brereton (1935), Chapter 2, 'Static Religion'.

The Bellman Confides in Her: first published in *PN Review*, July–August 2009.

Fisher, Roy, '"They Are All Gone Into the World": Roy Fisher in Conversation with Peter Robinson', in *Interviews Through Time, and Selected Prose*, ed. Tony Frazer (2000).

Lister, R., and others, *Samuel Palmer, A Vision Recaptured: The Complete Etchings and the Paintings for Milton and for Virgil* (1978).

Palmer, Samuel, letter to L.R. Valpy, June 1864, in Palmer, A.H., *The Life and Letters of Samuel Palmer, Painter and Etcher* (1892).

Vaughan, William and others, *Samuel Palmer 1805–1881: Vision and Landscape* (2005).

Di Fronte: first published in *PN Review*, March–April 2010.

Stokes, Adrian, *Venice: An Aspect of Art* (1945), Plate 18, San Sebastiano.

At South Elmham Minster: first published in *PN Review*, November–December 2010.

Journal, 13 July 2004.

Fairclough, John, and Mike Hardy, *Thornham and the Waveney Valley: A Historic*

Landscape Explored (2004), Plate 13.

Graham, Keith, *Hares* (1995).

Stokes, Adrian, 'On Resignation', in *A Game That Must Be Lost: Collected Papers*, ed. Eric Rhode (1973).

To a Nightingale: first published in *London Review of Books*, 18 November 2010.

Journal, 6 May and 26 June 2010.

Appendix: Contents of Individual Volumes
by R.F. Langley

Hem (London: *infernal methods*, 1978)
Matthew Glover
Saxon Landings
Blithing
The Ecstasy Inventories

Sidelong (Cambridge: *infernal methods*, 1981)
Juan Fernandez
Rough Silk
The Long History of Heresy

Twelve Poems (Cambridge: *infernal methods*, 1994)
Man Jack
Mariana
The Upshot
The Ecstasy Inventories
Juan Fernandez
Matthew Glover
Saxon Landings
Arbor Low
The Long History of Heresy
Blithing
Rough Silk
The Gorgoneion

Jack (Cambridge: Equipage, 1998)
Man Jack
Jack's Pigeon
The Barber's Beard
Tom Thumb
Poor Moth

Collected Poems (Manchester: Carcanet/*infernal methods*, 2000)
Mariana
The Upshot
The Ecstasy Inventories
Juan Fernandez
Matthew Glover
Saxon Landings
Arbor Low
The Long History of Heresy
Blithing
Rough Silk
The Gorgoneion
Man Jack
Jack's Pigeon

The Barber's Beard
Tom Thumb
Poor Moth
The Night Piece

More or Less (London: The Many Press, 2002)
Cakes and Ale
Cook Ting
Experiment with a Hand Lens
No Great Shakes
Still Life with Wineglass
Sixpence a Day
After the Funeral

Twine (Norwich: Landfill, 2004)
Depending on the Weather
Blues for Titania

The Face of It (Manchester: Carcanet, 2007)
Cakes and Ale
Cook Ting
Experiment with a Hand Lens
Sixpence a Day
Still Life with Wineglass
No Great Shakes
After the Funeral
Depending on the Weather
Blues for Titania
My Moth: My Song
Cash Point
Touchstone
Brute Conflict
Skrymir's Glove
At Sotterley
The Bellini in San Giovanni Crisostomo
Birdwatching Poem
Il Redentore
The Wall Tomb of Giacomo Surian
Achilles
Spoken Soon

Index of Titles

Index of First Lines